personality

personality

JULIAN B. ROTTER
University of Connecticut

DOROTHY J. HOCHREICH
University of Connecticut

Scott, Foresman and Company   Glenview, Illinois
Dallas, Tex.   Oakland, N.J.   Palo Alto, Cal.   Tucker, Ga.
Brighton, England

To
Sophia and Jack Hochreich
and
Saul, Norman, and Frances Rotter

Library of Congress Catalog Number: 74-16972
ISBN: 0-673-05268-0
Copyright © 1975
   Scott, Foresman and Company.
Philippines Copyright 1975
   Scott, Foresman and Company.
All Rights Reserved.
Printed in the United States of America.

Foreword

Both the content and the format of the beginning course in psychology vary widely today, not only between institutions and departments but also between instructors within the same department. There is a range of acceptable possibilities for organizing the course and considerable freedom for the instructor to select and emphasize those aspects of modern psychology which he or she considers most important and useful. One of the major reasons for course differences is the variety of subject matter and topics that are grouped under psychology. It is impossible to give adequate treatment to all the relevant topics within the time limitations typically imposed on the introductory course. To make matters more complicated, the accumulation of knowledge is proceeding at such a rapid pace in the different areas of psychology that it is virtually impossible for anyone to keep pace with new developments in all these fields. Thus, instructors often rightfully limit their treatment to those topics which they feel competent to present with knowledge and understanding. Finally, the current emphasis, in response largely to student and public demand, on the uses of psychology, on its relevance, must be noted. To be sure, not all instructors are convinced of the appropriateness of teaching the application of psychology in the beginning course, pointing to the potential dangers of a little knowledge and of premature attempts to use information not well-tested or standardized. In contrast, however, many who teach the introductory course give considerable time and attention to the application and the meaning of what is known.

With this variety in content, technique, and orientation among instructors, there is need for a corresponding variety of textual material. The Scott, Foresman Basic Psychological Concepts Series has been prepared in response to that need. Each title within the Series addresses a single topic. While the volumes are relatively brief, each gives a more intensified development of the topic than is available in any omnibus introductory textbook. Each volume has been prepared by an expert, who presents not only full knowledge of the current substantive and methodological state of his or her field, but who also provides an original and creative treatment of this material. The books are more than the typical cut-and-dried survey of a topic. There is room in each for the kind of original analysis of the problem heretofore unavailable in introductory reading.

Each title in the Series is independent of the others. They all have been written as a whole so as to maximize the coverage of psychology with minimal overlap and redundancy. No single title is a prerequisite to any other in the Series. In addition, we should note that there is considerable cross-referencing among the volumes and a general attempt at integrating facts and theories that are pertinent to several topics. While the titles are independent and may be used alone, they are also part of a larger, coordinated, comprehensive survey and interpretation of psychology.

The purpose of the Series is to provide both flexibility and expertise for the instructor and the student in the beginning course. The Series is adaptable to a variety of educational goals. Teachers can select and construct a set of reading units, with the content, emphasis, and sequence they desire and that will fit the general purpose and orientation of this course. They may, for example, base their course on several selected topics, each of which is developed in a separate volume. Alternatively, they may use only a single volume to fill a void or to further develop a topic of special importance. Volumes from the Series may be used in conjunction with most general textbooks. It is furthermore conceivable that one or another of the volumes would be useful in advanced courses, as preliminary reading for the student ill-prepared to contend with a topic on that level or as a supplement developing the background in a related topic. Because of the distinguished authorship of this Series, teachers can feel confident in their selection without fear of uneven quality, superficiality, or duplication. This Series has a variety of uses at different educational levels, depending upon the needs of the student, the purpose of the course, and the creativity and imagination of the instructor.

In the present volume, *Personality*, Julian Rotter and Dorothy Hochreich provide an admirable and representative survey of the ideas and research in the study of human personality. Personality theories are generally concerned with the persistent qualities of individuals, the characteristics that they carry with them that influence what they think and do and that differentiate them from other people. Needless to say, all sorts of conceptions have been advanced regarding the origin and operation of these abiding personal characteristics. Rotter and Hochreich give the reader an excellent introduction to the major formulations. Succinctly but clearly, they show how most of the leading theorists in this field have analyzed the development and functioning of the personality, what problems they have encountered, and what contributions they have made. The authors also review some of the techniques researchers employ in their investigations of personality and summarize their findings in several important areas. All in all, this volume offers a brief but fascinating tour through one of the main fields of psychology.

Lyle E. Bourne, Jr., Series Editor, University of Colorado
Leonard Berkowitz, Series Editor, University of Wisconsin

Preface

In this book we have attempted to introduce the student to the three most important aspects of personality study: representative theories, empirical data, and techniques of measurement. First, we have presented a selection of theories which have influenced the thoughts of many psychologists. But we have done more than merely describe these theories; we have tried to acquaint the student with the ways in which these theories can be compared and evaluated when approached from different points of view. We have, in other words, provided the student with the tools to understand and evaluate not only the theories presented in this book, but other theories as well.

Second, we have presented several areas of empirical investigation to acquaint the student with the kind of data typical of personality study, how these data are obtained, and how the data may relate to theoretical hypotheses. In doing so, we have chosen to describe specific experimental investigations in detail so that the student will be able to see how the data were collected, why the study was done, and the different interpretations that can be applied to the findings. In some cases, this approach will serve to illustrate how theory and research can go hand in hand.

Third, we have presented the student with a survey of both the kinds of instruments used to measure personality and the problems associated with measurement in general so that he or she can better understand the data of personality study. Rather than merely describing many tests which purport to measure personality characteristics, we have included discussions of the general problem of measurement and the advantages and disadvantages of different approaches to measurement.

In order to include all three important aspects of the study of personality in a brief introduction to the field, it was necessary to be selective; and it was impossible to include everything which may be interesting or relevant. We have, however, chosen those theories and empirical approaches which are representative of the field of personality study, past and present. Our own bias is toward the social learning theory of personality discussed in Chapter 8. Authors with other theoretical points of view would probably have selected differently.

We are indebted to Mrs. Mary Davis for her invaluable assistance in the preparation of the manuscript for this book.

Julian B. Rotter
Dorothy J. Hochreich
Storrs, Connecticut

Table of Contents

1

The Study
of Personality

The study of personality is a difficult and complex undertaking involving a variety of techniques, approaches, and ways of conceptualizing human nature and human behavior. Before we begin to explore some of the roads traveled by personality psychologists past and present, we must first try to define what we mean by "personality," the purposes of personality study, and the nature of personality theory.

In colloquial usage, the word "personality" is often treated as a global entity, and often as something that a given person has or doesn't have — for example, "She's got a lot of personality," or "He has an offensive personality." Psychologists, however, are more likely to talk about people in terms of specific characteristics or interrelated sets of characteristic ways of dealing with the world.

Many writers of textbooks in this field have spent pages discussing the question, "What is personality?" It is clear that multiple definitions of the term exist and that different psychologists regard personality in somewhat different ways. Most typically, however, the term is used to refer to the individual's characteristic, relatively stable ways of thinking, experiencing, and behaving, excluding only those stable characteristics which fall under the heading of intelligence or intellectual skills (i.e., those behaviors which are measured by means of standardized tests of general intelligence, achievement, or aptitude). In this book, "personality" will be regarded as a construct, a term used to designate certain *aspects* of people's behavior, and not as an entity.

THE PURPOSES OF PERSONALITY STUDY

Throughout history, every culture has developed a variety of ways for describing people—for communicating what someone is like. Such attempts to describe people can be regarded as the first of four major purposes for studying personality. One obvious way of describing a person is to note his physical characteristics; he is tall or short, heavy or slender, imposing or likely to pass unnoticed in a crowd. These are surface characteristics which are easy to perceive and to verify. But usually, we go beyond cataloging those characteristics which can be seen and include other characteristics which have to be inferred or guessed at on the basis of what someone has done or said. Thus, one might say of his closest friend that he is warm, fairly ambitious, outgoing, sensitive to others' feelings, and often nervous. All of these adjectives presumably have meaning to the listener; he, too, has known people whom he might describe in similar terms. And hopefully, although not necessarily, the words "warm," "ambitious," and "nervous" have more or less the same meaning for the speaker and listener, and the communication can, therefore, serve its purpose. The list of adjectives used to describe what are commonly known as personality characteristics is varied, extensive, and ever changing. (The "good guy" of your father's youth might have been called "neat" by your older brother, while you might describe him as "cool" or "together.")

Each of us is aware of a certain satisfaction we gain in being able to communicate our impressions to others, impressions which we often use in trying to explain our own actions and responses in various situations. Beyond this, there seem to be three other purposes which are often served by such descriptions in our everyday lives.

Suppose that you are about to choose one of several available literature courses, each of which sounds potentially interesting to you. Your friend knows something about the professors in that department, so you ask her what they're like. She describes one of the teachers as "stern," one as "egotistical," and one as "overly eager to please." How do you then use this information in making your decision? Assuming that you trust her judgment in such matters, you will try to predict how each professor will run his class and how his personal style is likely to affect your enjoyment of the course. Your reasoning might go as follows: "A stern teacher like Professor X is probably quite demanding, keeps his distance from students, is available to them only by special appointment, and hasn't much of a sense of humor. Professor Y, who is de-

scribed as egotistical, is most likely concerned only with his own knowledge and opinions, will expect students to merely 'spit back' his notes
on examinations without including any of their own ideas, and will tend
to view students' questions with disdain or see them as a threat. And
Professor Z, who is so eager to please students, is likely to be a 'marsh-
mallow' whose class will have little structure; he may tell a lot of jokes,
try to act younger than he is, and give in whenever a student appears to
disagree with his ideas, so that students probably learn very little in his
class." Having thought through the matter in this way, you will proceed
to choose one of the courses on the basis of your predictions about the
behaviors you anticipate from each of these men, predictions based on
the words your friend used in describing them. Psychologists engaged in
the study of personality are attempting, in a more formal and scientific
manner, to do essentially the same thing: to predict individual differences in the behavior of persons under similar conditions or in the same
kind of situation.

To illustrate the third purpose, let's assume that you have been married for a year or so and are about to have your first child. Like most
expectant parents, you and your wife or husband spend a good deal of
time thinking about how you should best bring up your son or daughter.
Looking back on your own childhood and adolescence, you see yourself
as very often confused and angry; you can remember many times when
you didn't know what to do or whom to believe, and you often acted
recklessly or foolishly as a result. Trying to determine why you had be-
haved this way, you think about your relationship with your parents.
What strikes you most readily about their responses to you through the
years is their inconsistency in matters of discipline, their disagreements
whenever a decision concerning their children had to be made. Asking
permission to do something, buy something, or go somewhere, you
could almost always be certain that your mother would say "yes" and
your father "no" or vice versa. If you attribute your frequent confusion
and anger to these parental behaviors (regardless of whether or not this
was the "true" or only cause), then you are making a kind of backward
prediction about how such uncomfortable feelings, and the behaviors
that express or accompany them, are acquired. On the basis of this post
hoc analysis of your earlier situation, you will make a prediction. You
will predict that the more consistent you and your spouse are in dealing
with your child, the less likely the child is to grow up experiencing anger and confusion and you will vow to act in accordance with this belief — for example, to always try to discuss problems together before mak-

ing decisions and communicating them to your child. This, too, is a major goal of personality psychologists: to attempt to understand or predict precisely how certain characteristic behaviors and attitudes are learned in the course of development.

The fourth purpose for studying personality is to determine how to change people's behavior. In order to do this, one must first arrive at an understanding of why a given behavior occurs. Imagine that living in your dormitory or apartment house were two women who did not get along well with each other, although both of them were good friends of yours. The situation was distressing to you and you wanted very much to bring them together. You thought back to the first time they met and remembered what happened on that occasion. Marlene, very attractive and self-assured, started to talk about her great social life—not showing off exactly, but just expressing her understandable pleasure at all the attention she was receiving. Barbara, less outgoing in social situations, seemed to feel that she had nothing to contribute to the conversation and simply withdrew without saying a word. Their subsequent encounters were similar in that Barbara, despite your attempts to include her in discussions, would remain silent as long as Marlene was present. Although Marlene did not seem to be aware of the effect she was having, it appeared obvious to you that Barbara felt that someone as popular as Marlene couldn't possibly be interested in her. Assuming that you had correctly assessed the situation, your next task was to figure out how to change the behaviors you regarded as damaging a potential set of friendships: Marlene's tendency to get so caught up in her own conversations that, without meaning to, she ignored Barbara, and Barbara's withdrawal whenever she was with Marlene. Since you thought it clear that Marlene's behavior was the cause of Barbara's withdrawal, you explained this to Marlene and persuaded her to draw Barbara out purposefully when they next met, to arrange a shopping expedition with Barbara, and in other ways to react to Barbara as a person rather than as just a silent listener. Your purpose here was to understand and predict not only how certain behaviors (such as Barbara's withdrawal) were acquired, but also how people's behaviors change. This concern with the explanation of behavior change is the fourth purpose of psychologists in studying personality.

In summary, the four major purposes of a personality theory are: (1) to develop ways of describing individuals in a reliable and useful fashion, (2) to understand and predict individual differences in people's behaviors or attitudes in similar situations, (3) to understand and predict how, or under what conditions, individuals learn or acquire their characteristic behaviors and attitudes, and (4) to understand how, or under what conditions, such behaviors and attitudes change. Psychologists' success in achieving their goals and in learning to make reasonably accurate predictions should result in new knowledge which could be profitably used to improve our methods of child-rearing and socialization, introduce more successful techniques of helping people to be happier and more productive through psychotherapy, and creating or modifying social institutions in ways which are better adapted to meet human needs.

THE NATURE OF PERSONALITY THEORY

Psychological Constructs

Scientific terms or concepts, which are the building blocks of psychological theories, are often referred to as *constructs*. The use of this word implies quite accurately that the descriptive terms used by psychologists and other scientists are "constructed" or made up in order to describe certain events which occur in nature. If we were to bring someone into a kennel and ask him to describe what he found there, he could do so in a number of ways. On the most general level, he might say that he saw ten animals, or, somewhat more specifically, ten dogs—that is, he might attend to the fact that they were living creatures and that they belonged to a particular animal species. What other characteristics might he attend to? Well, he might note that some of them were heavy and some were light, and describe them in terms of their weight. Or he might say that six were puppies and four were full grown, if their age struck him as being descriptively important. In each case, the terms used to describe the events encountered dealt with *aspects* of the events, not with the events themselves. The terms *heavy* and *light, puppy* and *full grown* are *relative* terms; they are not absolute properties of the objects, but have meaning only in relationship to other objects.

In addition, people with different purposes in mind will pay attention to different aspects of a given object or event. If one were describing a dog acquired primarily to be entered in dog shows and win blue ribbons, one would note its pedigree, height, weight, and color, but that would be just the beginning. One would also have to be concerned with the quality of its coat, its gait and posture, its breadth at shoulder and rear, the length and positions of its ears, and a number of other precisely cataloged characteristics. If, on the other hand, one were describing a house pet, one might say that it is a medium-sized, friendly springer spaniel pup, without further detailing characteristics which seem important to other kinds of dog owners.

A construct, then, is an abstraction of some aspect of an event made from a particular point of view. Constructs range from specific to very general and serve various purposes for the people who use them.

CONSTRUCT

Until now, we have been talking about constructs primarily as terms used to describe events which can be easily seen or measured. Constructs, however, not only are used to describe events but often represent attempts to explain certain happenings. For example, various kinds of explanations have been used to attempt to understand why it is that in most communities there are some people who behave strangely and do not conform to the norms of the community. Long ago, a person who was seen walking down the village streets talking to himself or to other people who were obviously not present, was said to be possessed by demons. As times changed, the same behavior was no longer explained as the result of a devil taking up residence within a person's brain, but as the result of some kind of "mental illness." It was reasoned that if physical abnormalities were the result of physical illness or disease, then mental abnormalities must likewise result from some disease process. In recent years, many people who are concerned about mental health have disagreed with this explanatory concept. They have pointed out that while it is possible to see and to measure organic disease processes, one cannot do likewise for most of the so-called "mental illnesses" that plague us. In the absence of valid evidence of actual organic abnormalities, many psychologists and psychiatrists today explain strange or maladaptive behaviors as attempts on the part of troubled people to cope with difficult life situations.

There are three lessons concerning constructs to be learned from this example. One, just because someone uses a term in trying to explain an event does not necessarily mean this term mirrors something that is "real." Two, a construct, whether or not it is valid and can be supported by substantial evidence, may serve the purpose of accounting for an event which is likely to be influenced by the explanatory concept one uses. If you explain peculiar behavior by attributing it to the presence of a demon, then you will try to "cure" the afflicted person by trying to exorcise the demon; or you might conclude that no cure is possible and simply get rid of the person by killing him or locking him up indefinitely. On the other hand, if you view such behavior as a symptom of mental illness or as a person's inadequate attempts to cope with a difficult situation, you would be more likely to hospitalize and treat the person, or to work at changing his life conditions in some way.

How the scientist decides when it is necessary to modify a construct in his theory, or even discard it altogether, will be discussed in detail in Chapter 2. But it should be noted here that, in all sciences, terms which at one time have been used to explain events of concern to the scientist are later rejected as being inadequate or erroneous in their implications. In the scientific study of any kind of event, the question we must ask is not, "What is this really?" but rather, "What is the most useful way of describing this event?" In asking the latter question, the scientist is committing himself to do away with earlier conceptions and replace them with new ones whenever they prove to be in error or not useful scientifically.

Criteria for Constructs: Reliability and Utility

There are two major criteria by means of which one can judge the value of constructs. The first of these is reliability, or measurability. By reliability we mean the degree to which the same event, observed by a number of different scientists, would be described in the same way by all of them. If a psychologist believes that highly intelligent people are more likely to plan for the future than are less intelligent people, he must specify exactly what he means by "highly intelligent" and "less intelligent." He must first define the construct "intelligence" in abstract language (the *ideal definition*) and then specify the intelligence test he used as a measure and the exact cut-off scores he used in separating his highly intelligent and less intelligent subjects. This specification of the method used in measuring the construct is called the *operational definition*. In defining intelligence as a person's score on the Wechsler Adult Intelligence Scale, one is specifying the exact operations used to measure the construct. This allows a psychologist to communicate precisely what he means in objective terms so that others working in the same area of interest can understand, verify (or refute), and build on his findings. Psychologists working with personality variables often use constructs for which there is no measure as widely accepted as are some standardized intelligence tests. While we must move in the direction of developing better operational definitions of our personality constructs and be prepared to discard mediocre definitions for better ones as we develop more accurate measurement tools, it is still possible to seek temporary solutions to the problem of reliability by using carefully chosen behavioral examples to illustrate what we mean by a construct.

The second criterion for a good construct is its *utility* for a given purpose. Utility refers to the degree to which a construct enables us to understand how some event came to be, what conditions gave rise to the event, and/or what predictions we can make about the future. "Intelligence," defined as a person's score on an intelligence test, is very useful in predicting how a child is likely to do in a public school. It may be less useful or not at all useful if what one wishes to predict is this child's future success in industry or business. In the latter case, an individual who tends to achieve a fairly low score on standard tests of intelligence but who is very adept at evaluating people to determine what they want and how much they are willing to pay for it may be likely to do better in the business world than the person who has a high I.Q. but who does not have this particular kind of ability. We could call this ability "intelligence," too, but we would have to define and measure it quite differently. Thus, a construct may be scientifically useful for one purpose but not for another.

2

Dimensions of Personality Theories

Since one major purpose of this book is to examine a number of representative theories of personality, it would seem useful at this point for the reader to have some tools which he might use for assessing and comparing these theories. Just as the personality theorist, in observing an infinite variety of behaviors, must decide upon what aspects of human behavior seem most important for him to focus upon, so, too, must the student of personality make decisions about which aspects of theories are most important and useful in allowing him to arrive at intelligent evaluations.

In this chapter, six dimensions will be presented as potentially useful ways of looking at personality theories. The use of the term *dimension* implies the notion of a continuum along which one might order a number of theories, rather than describing them in an "either-or" or "black-white" fashion.

Three of the dimensions discussed are concerned with the formal characteristics of the theory itself. These are the (a) systematic versus nonsystematic, (b) operational versus nonoperational, and (c) content versus process dimensions.

The other three dimensions involve the ways in which various theories deal with the question of individual differences in personality characteristics. These are the (a) constitution and heredity versus experience, (b) generality versus specificity, and (c) internal versus situational dimensions.

In addition to considering theories in terms of this kind of dimensional analysis, there are two important questions which might be asked about each theory we study: (a) "What are the assumptions, implicit or explicit, regarding the nature of motivation or the directional quality of human behavior?" and (b) "How is personality change explained by the theory?"

FORMAL DIMENSIONS

Systematic Versus Nonsystematic

A theory may be viewed as an attempt to organize a selected body of observations, data, and ideas. Theories in psychology can vary from a loose collection of statements about certain behaviors or events to a tightly organized series of propositions which interrelate a set of constructs and allow for precise mathematical predictions. While it is currently not feasible to talk about such mathematical properties in regard to the complex area of personality study, the theories which we shall discuss in the chapters to follow do vary greatly in their degree of systematization.

One major defining characteristic of a good or ideal system is that everything is made explicit. The theory should, for example, specify the phenomena, events, or aspects of events to which the system applies. Essentially, this means that the theorist defines his "territory" and accepts responsibility for his attempts to explain or predict behaviors that fall within his stated area of concentration. Similarly, the underlying assumptions or givens of a system should be stated explicitly. This is an especially important requirement in the case of personality theories, in which the theorist's personal values and notions about human nature may be unintentionally masqueraded as scientific facts.

A second important characteristic of a good theory has to do with the ways in which its constructs are linked together. In our earlier discussion, we spoke of constructs as the building blocks of a theory. The theories of personality which we shall be studying vary not only in terms of the quality of their basic constructs, but also in terms of how these constructs are related to each other.

A system usually involves constructs or concepts at several levels of abstraction. Direct observations of events are used to define lower-level constructs, and the lower-level constructs are used in turn to define higher-level constructs. A tightly organized system is one in which con-structs are linked with other constructs at the same level and at different levels of abstraction, and the direction of the relationships between or among constructs is specified.

For example, Freud observed in a number of the patients he was treating certain behaviors which were both distressing themselves and were clearly interfering with the patients' normal everyday functioning. Some patients reported that they felt compelled to repeat over and over again certain thoughts and/or ritualized behaviors, such as washing their hands, checking to be sure they had locked all their doors, or turning their pillow innumerable times before retiring. As Freud's clinical experience with such cases grew, he decided that all of these observable behaviors might be described as obsessive-compulsive symptoms (lower-level construct). He called them "symptoms" because these behaviors seemed to be exaggerations of normally realistic behaviors engaged in by most people, and because the need to repeat these acts was painful to the patients. His medical training led Freud to view these behaviors as "signs" of some underlying disturbance, in the same way that physicians view reports of chronic indigestion as signs of some sort of organic disturbance involving the gastrointestinal system.

Thus, the goal of Freud's treatment procedures was to discover the source of the underlying disturbance which was producing the clearly maladaptive symptoms. From his interviews with these patients, he learned that any attempts on their part to *not* do what they felt compelled to do resulted in their feeling extremely fearful and upset. Freud labeled these feelings "neurotic anxiety," defined as a fearful response to events which were not generally considered dangers by most people. He suggested that the obsessive-compulsive symptoms (lower-level construct) enabled the patients to "ward off" the anxiety (intermediate-level construct). As long as the patients continued to engage in these repetitive acts, they need not experience the intensely unpleasant feelings; the symptoms were seen as *defending* the patients against anxiety.

The next step for Freud was to try to discover the source or cause of the anxiety, assuming that if one could remove the anxiety, the symptoms would no longer be necessary and would therefore disappear. Studying the symbolic content of the patients' memories, dreams, free associations, and repetitive thoughts or behaviors, Freud collected evidence that led him to conclude that the anxiety was the result of unconscious sexual conflicts. Specifically, he suggested that the superego (conscience) of his patients was overly dominant and so had prevented the full development of the ego (that part of mental functioning which he thought of as mediating between the demands of instinctual needs, conscience, and the external world). Here, he established a link between two high-level constructs, with the direction of the relationship specified. His further suggestion that a weak ego and a strong superego lead to a high degree of anxiety, and that anxiety results in symptoms which represent defenses against anxiety, specifies and interrelates constructs at three levels of abstraction. Thus, what we see in Freud's system (at least in this part of the system) is a set of interrelated constructs, with higher-level abstractions "anchored" to observations by a series of lower-level constructs.

Some of the theories which we shall be studying are characterized by an absence of constructs at some level(s) of abstraction, and their predictive power is thereby weakened in certain respects. If a theory lacks higher-level constructs, then less generality is present. If the lower-level constructs are missing or are not made sufficiently explicit, then it becomes extremely difficult to test the hypotheses or relationships posited among the higher-level constructs.

A third characteristic of a good theory is that attempts are made to specify time relationships. If a theorist, for example, is focusing upon the particular construct, anxiety, he should suggest (testable) hypotheses about those conditions which precede the onset of anxiety (antecedent conditions such as overly strict childrearing practices, traumatic events, etc.) and those conditions which are likely to follow anxiety in time (consequent conditions such as defensive behaviors, reduced ability to concentrate, disturbed interpersonal relationships, etc.).

While too few constructs present a problem in some theories, others may be inefficient because of too many overlapping constructs. For example, in some of the theories of psychopathology, the antecedent conditions which lead to disturbed functioning are presumed to be the same for many different disorders; and the disorders themselves are characterized by many overlapping symptoms. The results are an unreliability of diagnosis and an inefficiency of prediction. A fourth characteristic of a good theory, then, is that overlapping constructs (those which are defined very similarly and/or those with the same antecedents or consequences) are eliminated.

There are theorists who disagree with some of these yardsticks for measuring the adequacy of a theory and who believe that the stating of precise relationships limits the development of a theory. In our view, however, the explicit statement of relationships among constructs has many advantages.

One advantage is that in tackling a new problem, the theorists usually find it possible to deduce a hypothesis or to make a prediction. In other words, more systematic theories not only lead to research but also focus the direction of research; this is more orderly and efficient than approaching problems by means of a trial-and-error procedure.

A second advantage of a system is that once the appropriate research is done and empirical observations obtained, one is able to test a general proposition or a series of general propositions, so that the generality or utility of the findings is increased considerably.

The third advantage of a system is that increased prediction can result from a single observation or a limited number of observations. If, for example, a concept such as strength of a need for achievement is linked systematically to many other constructs, then the single measure of the strength of this need will permit the making of a great many related predictions. The more systematic the linkages of a specific construct, the more predictions can be obtained from a single measurement.

In summary, the following characteristics define a more complete and adequate system:

(1) Assumptions, givens, and the phenomena or events to which the system applies are explicitly stated.

(2) The constructs are linked together into a network with the direction of the relationships between (among) the constructs specified. Broad principles or hypotheses relating higher-level abstractions are anchored to observations by a series of lower-level constructs.

(3) As much as possible, time relationships are specified so that constructs are anchored both by antecedent conditions and consequent conditions.

(4) Overlapping constructs are eliminated to increase efficiency of prediction and reliability of measurement.

Operational Versus Nonoperational

In order to be useful, a theory should lend itself to empirical test so that hypotheses, having been tested, may be accepted as valid, modified, or rejected entirely. This is possible when the terms or constructs used in the theory are defined operationally. An operational definition is a definition of a construct which describes how the construct is measured. The degree of operationality of the theory refers to the extent to which operations for measuring its constructs are specified or ways of developing such operations are suggested.

There are a number of criteria for good operations for measurement of constructs. First, they should be *reliable,* as pointed out in Chapter 1. Different scientists should be able to measure the same variable under the same circumstances and come up with the same results. Second, the operations should be *logically consistent with the ideal or common sense definition of the construct.* If operations are not logically consistent with the definition, other scientists would be unable to clearly understand one's research findings, and these findings might not provide an adequate test of the hypothesis under consideration. Third, a good operation should be *specific to a particular construct.* If your theory leads you to hypothesize that anxiety and self-esteem are related but different constructs, then you would have to devise different operations for measuring each of these constructs in order to then test the hypothesis that they are related but not identical. Fourth, an operation should be as *quantitatively precise as possible.* This allows for more exact and accurate prediction of behavior. Fifth, an operation should, of course, be *practically possible,* or it would be of no use at all. And sixth, an operation should be based on *explicitly designated observables.* If all the constructs in a theory refer to internal "feeling states" which cannot be directly observed and are not related in the theory to specific observable behaviors, their operations would be difficult to achieve. The fact that a theorist has devised operations for some of his theoretical constructs does not make his theory a good one unless the operations at least approach these six criteria. Contemporary psychologists tend to be more concerned with problems of measurement or operationality than were most of the earlier personality theorists. And, as we shall see in later chapters, there have been recent attempts to operationalize constructs suggested by some of these earlier theorists.

Content Versus Process

One major purpose of any theory of personality is to understand how individuals acquire and change their characteristic behavior patterns. A process theory is designed to fulfill this goal—that is, to explain or specify (a) the relationship of prior events (such as specific childhood experiences, family dynamics, or environmental factors) to later behaviors, and

(b) the conditions necessary for a change in behavior to occur. In other words, that part of a theory which we refer to as the process part concerns itself with answering the questions of *how* people come to be as they are and *how* they change in various ways.

A second major purpose of a personality theory is to understand, predict, or describe individual differences. To satisfy this purpose, one needs a *content theory*, a theory which specifies the useful descriptive terms which characterize the more general and consistent kinds of human behavior. Here the theorist is concerned with *what* behaviors or categories of human behavior are important and should be focused upon in order to allow for prediction of individual differences in behavior in a variety of significant life situations.

In point of fact, what we are discussing here are two dimensions, rather than a single dimension. It is possible for a theory to be high or low on either or both dimensions. A learning theory which specifies how behaviors are acquired and how they change, but does not group or categorize different kinds of behaviors, would be a process theory lacking content. At the opposite extreme, a theory which only describes some number of basic personality types and their characteristic behaviors without specifying how these behaviors evolve or change would be a content theory lacking in process relationships. Clearly, a theory which provides both process laws and content categories is potentially the most useful. A theory deficient in either process or content is likely to be weak in one or the other of the major areas of prediction.

INDIVIDUAL DIFFERENCES DIMENSIONS

Heredity and Constitution Versus Experience

Theories differ in the extent to which they emphasize the importance of hereditary and constitutional factors versus learning and experiential factors in their explanations of individual personality differences.

There are certain logical consequences of explaining the presence of particular ways of behaving on the basis of genetic inheritance or constitution, and these consequences may be seen as limiting the personality theorist in several ways. If one assumes genetic and constitutional determinants to be of central importance, then one is also likely to assume (a) a strong consistency in behavior over time, and (b) a relatively great limitation on the potential for change through experience. In other words, an individual's experiences in life are seen as unlikely to affect or change his behavior in major ways because of built-in mechanisms (e.g., in-stincts, constitutional predispositions) which predispose him to react to his environment in a certain fashion.

A theorist who embraces such assumptions is likely to place relatively little emphasis upon understanding how experience can change people; and such an orientation as this tends to lack process laws stating how individuals acquire characteristic modes of behavior. Questions dealing with acquisition tend rather to be relegated to other fields, such as genetics and physiology. Prediction, as a result, is extremely limited. Making assumptions regarding antecedent conditions only after a pattern of behavior has appeared does not constitute a useful scientific explanation. And this approach may also limit the degree to which a theory is likely to lead to new knowledge regarding personality change and methods of psychotherapy.

Theories which emphasize the influence of learning and experience involve a different kind of limitation. In discussing very early learning, they are unable to account for differences in response to what appear to be similar environmental conditions. In other words, the usefulness of the theory extends only so far back in time; some antecedents for early learning cannot be identified, and the theorist must accept some individual differences simply as givens.

A major advantage of the emphasis on experience or learning is that it provides a logical basis for relating hypotheses regarding acquisition of behaviors to hypotheses regarding change. The theorist is likely to specify process relationships, and such a theory tends to generate or lead to research hypotheses with implications for practical application of new knowledge. Presumably, if we can discover how various behaviors are learned (under what conditions a behavior appears and is maintained), then we can try to apply this knowledge to the goal of changing behaviors. Likewise, learning something about how behaviors are changed (in the course of everyday experience or within the context of special situations, such as psychotherapy), will lead us to specific hypotheses concerning how such behaviors were originally acquired. For example, we might discover that children who become extremely anxious in testing situations tend to come from families which set extremely high standards for achievement. If we knew that test-anxious children have experienced a great deal of parental pressure, we would have some good notions about how we might reduce this anxiety — that is, by having parents and teachers show greater acceptance and less criticism of such children's performance in school.

Generality Versus Specificity

Theories of personality vary in the degree to which they explain behavior in terms of one or a few broad general characteristics versus a larger number of specific and relatively independent traits or characteristic ways of responding.

The typological approach to personality provides a good example of the highly generalized approach. The typological view assumes that some single characteristic represents the "core" of the individual's personality and permeates everything he does. Since all of the person's characteristic behaviors are presumed to depend upon his "type," it should be quite easy, by observing or measuring his behavior in virtually any kind of situation, to determine which typological category he best fits. Once typed, a vast number of behavioral predictions would then be possible. This would provide great efficiency of prediction if, in fact, such systems were shown to be valid. However, this is not at all the case. The empirical data rarely support broad typologies as predictive. In those rare instances where support for typological hypotheses has been obtained, the level of predictions has been only slightly better than chance.

In addition, highly generalized systems usually do not provide any basis for understanding individual differences *within* a type category. If one divides the world up into introverts and extroverts, the very important differences in behavior among introverts (or among extroverts) cannot be determined by such a simplistic system. The same thing would be true if the world were divided into those with positive self-concepts and negative self-concepts, those who are self-actualized versus those who are not, and so on.

At the other extreme of the dimension, one could conceive of personality as being comprised of a large number of specific traits or potentials to respond in certain ways, all of them relatively independent and not bound together by broader, more generalized characteristics. Instead of describing an individual as being generally dependent upon others, for example, one could think of him as having a specific dependency rating in regard to all of the significant figures in his life. Using appropriate measures, it might be determined that he is dependent on his mother at the 60th percentile, on his father at the 30th, on his wife at the 40th, on his friends at the 10th, and so on. If each one of these characteristics were assessed carefully, the specific predictions would undoubtedly be more highly accurate than would predictions based on a generalized characteristic. It is certainly true that there is specificity in everyone's reactions to the different social stimuli and life situations he encounters. Let's take, as an example, two college students, Tom and Mike, whose friends describe them as being vastly different in terms of their interests, attitudes, beliefs, ambitions, sensitivity, and other characteristics. Even given these substantial personality differences between the two men, one would be likely to find that if Tom's behaviors were compared with Mike's behaviors in a classroom situation (or at a football game), they would be more similar than the behaviors of Tom in the classroom versus Tom at the game. Since, in our daily lives, we participate in a variety of specific and widely varying situations, the more a system of personality takes this specificity into account, the higher its level of prediction will be.

The problem, however, with this extremely specific approach lies in its lack of efficiency. To assess an individual's characteristics in this way would require an overwhelming number of measurements. And measuring characteristic A in situation X would not provide one with any basis for predicting the strength of characteristic A in situations Y or Z. While it is true that research in psychology demonstrates that an individual does react differentially to specific situations, there is also a vast literature indicating that varying degrees of generality exist in behavior. In fact, the problem of developing a useful and valid content theory is largely one of finding those constructs which best describe that generality which does exist, without assuming generality to be present when it is not.

In summary, either extreme of this dimension involves severe limitations. The too general approach to personality leads to erroneous predictions or is limited to a very low level of accuracy. The extreme position of specificity involves making a great many measurements in order to make predictions and the loss of efficiency from potential predictions based on valid generalized characteristics.

Internal Versus Situational

In the older views of personality, each person was considered to be a member of some type category, or perhaps several categories, and attempts were made to predict his behavior on the basis of this categorization. In describing an individual's personality it was not necessary to specify the circumstances or situations in which his behaviors occurred;

he didn't *act* in a given way in a particular kind of situation but, rather, he *had* a particular characteristic. Explanation of behavior, then, was done entirely in terms of an internal state, characteristic, type, trait, or disorder.

At the opposite extreme of the continuum, a purely situational approach would be one attempting to understand individual behavior entirely in terms of the differences in the situations in which individuals find themselves. This view would ignore internal variables such as the person's previous experiences.

A more sophisticated approach, favored by a number of contemporary psychologists, is one which stresses neither internal nor situational determinants to the exclusion of the other, but rather takes both kinds of variables into account in explaining behavior. This might be called an "interactional" view of personality. Thus, instead of suggesting that a person acts consistently across virtually all situations, or that there is little or no consistency in his behavior from one situation to another, this view suggests that there is *some* consistency in behavior; that is, the stability of an individual's behavior tends to be consistent for a particular kind or *class of situations*.

Internal versus situational determination of behavior is clearly related to the previously discussed dimension of generality versus specificity. However, this aspect of a theory can be independent of generality-specificity. A theory might list several hundred specific traits but never base prediction on the situation in which the person is acting. On the other hand, a theory might involve a few types whose behavior varied according to threatening versus nonthreatening situations, providing an interaction model but a highly general one.

Again, we find ourselves suggesting that adherence to either an extremely internal or an extremely situational approach is likely to be less useful than working with both kinds of variables within a single theory. We must attend to important distinguishing characteristics of various classes of situations as well as to the history of previous experiences of individuals, experiences which affect their perception of any meaningful life situation. What one individual finds stressful, another person does not. What is rewarding for one person is punishing for another. We might ask about any theory which attempts to predict behavior, "To what extent does it utilize both internal and situational determinants?" To the degree that it neglects either, prediction will be reduced accordingly.

MOTIVATIONAL ASSUMPTIONS

Almost every theory of personality recognizes the importance of direc-
tionality of behavior. The individual's behaviors or reactions are viewed
as attempts to change his environment in some way. The goal of human
behaviors may be conceptualized in a variety of ways; for example our
actions may be seen as attempts to satisfy basic drives, to maintain some
sort of psychological equilibrium, to meet physiological and psychological needs, to achieve self-actualization, and so on. Still other theorists
talk about motivation in terms of instincts or other forces not specifically
labeled, but all of which imply a natural direction to behavior which is
characteristic of the human species.

Differences in personality, from a motivational point of view, can be
described in terms of differences in the strength of drives, learned psychological needs, instincts, or other life forces. Individual differences
can also be explained in terms of the results of inhibition of any of these
assumed sources of motivation. To understand fully and evaluate any
personality theory, it is necessary to examine the motivational assumptions, implicit or explicit, and to assess the degree to which these assumptions lend themselves to empirical investigation.

PERSONALITY CHANGE

One major characteristic of human beings is their constant attempt to
improve themselves and their environment. By means of education, attempts to develop better childrearing practices, social action, and various forms of psychotherapy and remedial experiences, we strive to provide a better existence for ourselves and others.

One of the primary purposes underlying the development of personality theories has been the attempt to understand human behavior so that it
may be changed in ways which are more satisfying, productive, pleasurable, liberating, and so forth. Given the assumption that people do
achieve certain stable characteristics, how are changes accomplished?
When in the life cycle, if ever, do personality patterns achieve relative
stability? How much change is possible after stability has been achieved?
These questions are part of the general question of what is the process
underlying the development and change of personality characteristics. If
a theory has no clear-cut implications for how relatively stable characteristics can be changed once they have been acquired, then it lacks utility

for the broader problems of psychotherapy and for the more general questions of social change.

REPRESENTATIVE THEORIES OF PERSONALITY

The following six chapters provide descriptions of six theories of personality. In addition, five of the theories are analyzed with respect to the dimensions discussed above. There exist numerous theories of personality, only some of which will be sampled here. The classical psychoanalytic theory of Sigmund Freud and Alfred Adler's individual psychology have been chosen not only because they are still widely followed and applied to a variety of practical problems, but also because they have had a major influence upon contemporary theories which are generally categorized as neo-Freudian or neo-Adlerian.

Carl Rogers' theory has played an important role in psychotherapy practice and research. It may also be regarded as representative of those theories which emphasize subjective experience as the basic datum of psychology.

Along with Carl Rogers, Abraham Maslow's approach may be considered to be a representative of the many current theories that are regarded as humanistic or existential approaches to personality. While not as complete a theory as the others, a brief section on Erik Erikson has been included because of his focus on adolescence, an important period of life frequently neglected by other theorists.

Rotter's social learning theory has been selected as a representative of learning theory approaches because of its emphasis on the direct application of learning principles and its inclusion of a content theory also related to learning principles. This social learning theory is also the authors' orientation and acts as a bias in the choice of theories presented, in the method of analyzing those theories, and in the selection of empirical studies presented in Chapter 10.

3

Freud's Psychoanalysis

Beginning our discussion of representative theories of personality with Sigmund Freud (1938) is appropriate not only because his was the first major psychological theory aimed at understanding complex human behavior, but also because his work has influenced all subsequent approaches to the study of personality. Indeed the impact of his thinking has, through the years, extended into other disciplines and fields of interest such as anthropology, education, sociology, and literature.

It is difficult to describe or characterize psychoanalysis because the term means different things to different people. Many current theories (Horney, Sullivan, Jung, Fromm, Erikson) tend to be classified as psychoanalytic despite the fact that they have borrowed liberally from Adler, learning theory, sociology, and other sources. There is considerable variation among these theories in their closeness to classical, or orthodox, Freudian theory.

In addition to the application of the psychoanalytic label to many different theoretical positions, confusion also results from the fact that this term applies to three different kinds of statements. The first kind are those statements which refer to the observations of and inferences about human behavior made by Freud and his followers. These include inferences about the meaningfulness of *all* behaviors, including dreams, errors, and slips of the tongue; observations of the strong relationships often existing between parents and children of the opposite sex; the tendency of many people to "forget" unpleasant thoughts or events, and so forth. Many of these observations and inferences have been widely accepted as meaningful and important contributions to our knowledge of human behavior. The second kind of psychoanalytic statements or concepts are those which comprise Freud's theory of personality per se. And the third aspect of psychoanalysis includes statements about a method of psychotherapy or treatment of behavioral or emotional problems by means of specific techniques developed by Freud and his colleagues. Here, we are primarily concerned with the second aspect of psychoanalysis: the classical personality theory.

MAJOR ASSUMPTIONS

Basic to Freud's personality theory are two assumptions, both of which are widely regarded as major contributions to psychological thinking. The first is his principle of *psychic determinism*. Freud felt that human behavior was motivated or directed toward obtaining specific goals; all behavior, according to this principle, is believed to have meaning and purpose. This assumption clearly has far-reaching implications; it means that strange or "crazy" behaviors, or simple everyday occurrences such as slips of the tongue, dreams, and memory losses which have no obvious logical explanation, all have particular significance and may be interpreted or understood in the light of an individual's motives. In *The Psychopathology of Everyday Life* (1904), Freud recounts many common examples of errors and forgetting of names, words, and actions, all of which are viewed as instances of motivated behavior, rather than as simple accidents. Indeed the term *Freudian slip*, referring to a slip of the tongue which lends itself to some pointed, and perhaps embarrassing, interpretation, has by this time worked its way into our everyday language.

The second major assumption is that of *unconscious motivation*. While Freud was not the first man to recognize that people were not always aware of the purposes or motives for their behavior, this notion was given special emphasis in Freud's theory, especially during the early years of psychoanalysis. The task Freud set for himself was that of discovering the unconscious or unknown determining forces in personality. Assuming that all behaviors, overt (actions, language) or covert (thoughts, mental images) had meaning, and that the person was typically unaware of the motivation underlying many of his behaviors, the purpose of psychoanalytic study was to search for the meanings and thereby render the unconscious conscious. For Freud, there were three levels of consciousness. First, there is the *conscious* mind, which includes everything of which the person is aware. Second, there is the *preconscious*, which includes ideas or memories which are just below the level of awareness, and can become conscious quite easily. For example, we have all had the experience of trying to remember some name or event which is "just on the tip of the tongue." Usually we are able, in these instances, to recover the memory after thinking about it for awhile or just waiting until it comes back to us. Such relatively accessible memories are preconscious. The third, and least accessible or "deepest" level of consciousness is the unconscious. Freud compared the mind to an iceberg, with the conscious mind representing the tip of the iceberg, and the larger and more significant unconscious processes existing below the surface of awareness.

ENERGY AND INSTINCTS

Freud postulated a form of energy, psychic energy, which performs psychological work such as thinking and remembering, in the same sense that one speaks of physical energy doing physical work. This mental energy was presumed to derive from instincts. An instinct is an inherited, inborn condition which gives direction to behavior (Hall, 1954).

In Freudian theory, instincts are divided into two categories: *life instincts* (eros) and *death instincts* (thanatos). The life instincts are the mental representatives of all those bodily needs (hunger, thirst, sex, etc.) associated with survival of the individual and of the species. The sex instinct is the life instinct which is given the greatest prominence in psychoanalytic theory. The term *libido* is used to refer to the energy of the life instincts. The presumed ultimate goal of the death instincts (destructiveness and aggression) is the return of the organism to the inorganic state. This notion of death instincts (Freud, 1922) grew out of Freud's attempts to account for phenomena such as masochism and some people's apparent compulsion to repeat neurotic, self-destructive, or fruitless behaviors. Although the concept of death instincts has, to a large extent, fallen into disrepute among modern Freudian theorists, the instinctual approach itself has not been rejected by them. There are still attempts to explain behavior by relegating it to a hypothesized energy source that is presumed to be inherited, but that is not directly measurable or predictable. Questions such as why children around the age of six show considerable attachment to parents of the opposite sex, why people become aggressive following frustration, why many people are sexually attracted to persons of the same sex, and so on, are answered,

"They have inherited an energy source that directs them to do it." Freud did state that the particular behaviors by means of which the energy was expressed were perhaps a function of learning or experience; adult behaviors were thought to be greatly influenced by what happened to the person when these instinctual energies were expressed during early childhood. But for the ultimate "why" questions, Freud relied upon instinctual explanations.

THE STRUCTURE OF PERSONALITY

Behavior, for Freud, is determined by the interaction of three different systems or mind entities: the id, the ego, and the superego. When these three systems are working together harmoniously, the individual is said to be well adjusted; when there is discord among the systems, the person is maladjusted or is not functioning optimally.

The *id* is the system from which the ego and superego eventually become differentiated. Conceptualized as the source of the instincts and of psychic energy derived from instinctual needs, the id provides the motive force for the other two systems. In response to internal or external stimulation, energy increases within the id and is experienced as tension (discomfort or pain). When this occurs, the id functions so as to discharge the tension completely or, if this is not possible, to reduce it to a tolerable level. The id operates according to the *pleasure principle*; its aim is to avoid pain or discomfort and to seek pleasure or satisfaction. It attempts to accomplish this aim by means of *primary process thinking*. For example, an infant feeling the pangs of hunger but clearly incapable of going to the refrigerator for a glass of milk will produce a mental image of the desired object (mother's breast) in an effort to discharge the tension. Dreams are also considered to be examples of primary process thinking; for Freud, all dreams represent the person's primitive desires. Because primary process thinking is not effective in reducing tensions such as hunger, a new psychological process develops, one which is attuned to the demands and opportunities of the world of objective reality.

The *ego*, the second system of the personality, develops because of this need to deal with the real world in order to meet one's needs. It acts in accordance with the *reality principle*; its aim is to postpone the discharge of energy until it discovers an object which will satisfy the need. It does this by means of *secondary process* or realistic thinking, and thus incorporates the higher mental processes: reasoning, planning, judgment, and so forth. The ego functions as a kind of executive, in that it is responsible for balancing and integrating the demands of the id, the superego, and the external world.

The *superego* is the third system to develop and represents the values and ideals of the culture which are transmitted to the child through his parents with whom he identifies. The child is said to incorporate these standards of conduct through the process of introjection. The superego comprises two subsystems: the conscience and the ego-ideal. Those behaviors and attitudes which are disapproved and punished by the parents become incorporated into the conscience. Once these standards have been introjected, the conscience punishes the person by making him feel guilty for his transgressions. Those behaviors and attitudes which are admired and rewarded by the parents are introjected as the ego-ideal. Whenever the person lives up to these standards, the ego-ideal rewards him with feelings of pride and accomplishment. The development of the superego thus substitutes self-control for parental control; the child becomes capable of rewarding and punishing himself for good and bad behaviors.

In the well-functioning personality, these three process systems are presumed to work together as a team. The id seeks pleasure in the form of immediate gratification of needs, the superego seeks perfection in terms of meeting high moral standards, and the ego seeks to satisfy or balance the demands of the id and the superego within the bounds of what is realistically possible. Because there is only a certain amount of psychic energy available for psychological functioning, as one system gains energy or strength, the other two systems must necessarily become proportionately weaker (Hall, 1954). A too strong superego, for example, would mean that both the id and ego have been de-energized, and this would be reflected in unrealistic and rigid "good" behavior.

STAGES OF DEVELOPMENT

For Freud, the first five years of life were crucial in determining the individual's personality structure and functioning. Instincts were used to account for behavioral changes during early development, and a *theory of psychosexual development* was posited. The term "psychosexual" refers to the psychological aspects of the sexual instinct which is inborn and which Freud presumed to be related to organic drives. Freud's concept of the sexual instinct was broad and included the manipulation or use of *any* bodily zone for pleasure or satisfaction; by Freud's definition, then, *sexual* means *pleasurable*. He hypothesized that whereas a child starts out with an instinctual urge for one kind of sexual gratification, later on he will seek another kind. The object or bodily zone (erogenous zone) changes with development, but also tends to be affected by experience.

During the *oral stage*, which occurs during the first year of life, the infant seeks gratification by putting things in his mouth, sucking, (oral-erotic stage) and biting (oral-aggressive stage).

This is followed by the *anal stage*, during which the child's energies are focused upon eliminative functions in terms of "holding in" (anal-retentive stage) and "letting go" (anal-expulsive stage) of the body's waste products. This usually occurs during the second year of life, and the parents' attitudes and behaviors regarding toilet training are believed to have important consequences for personality development. It is when toilet training procedures are instituted that the child first experiences demands to postpone gratification and to exercise control over instinctual needs.

The third stage of development, the *phallic stage*, involves the child's focus on his sexual organs; he seeks pleasure through masturbation. It is during this stage, when the child is between three and five years old, that the *Oedipus complex* is said to develop, and these oedipal experiences are thought to be important in determining the person's later attitudes toward people of the opposite sex and toward authority figures. The Oedipus complex occurs somewhat differently for males and females. Both sexes, very early in life, are closer to the mother and love her more because she is their primary caretaker; the father is seen as a rival for the mother's attention. During the oedipal period, the boy experiences incestuous desires; he wishes to possess his mother and get rid of his father. Resenting the father and fantasizing his death or destruction, the boy develops a fear that his rival will destroy him by harming his genital organs. This is called *castration anxiety*. The fear of castration leads to repression of the child's sexual feelings toward his mother and hostility toward his father. The boy *identifies* with his father *(identification with the aggressor)*, emulates the father's behavior, and thereby comes to vicariously possess his mother — a compromise solution.

The female child's situation is presumed to be different. Her primary love object, formerly the mother, switches during the oedipal period. Freud posits that her discovery that males have penises evokes feelings of disappointment and envy *(penis envy)* in the little girl. Because she desires a penis, she desires her father who possesses this organ and resents her mother as a rival for her father's attention. So, whereas the boy fears that his penis will be taken away from him, the girl imagines that she has lost her penis and wishes to recover it. It is suggested by Freud that the lack of a penis is compensated for when a woman gives birth to a child, especially if it is a male child. The female Oedipus complex (sometimes called the *Electra complex*), unlike the boy's, tends to persist, although she identifies with her mother and thereby becomes closer to her father.

The above description of events presumed to occur during the oedipal period is complicated by Freud's assumption that every person is inherently bisexual—that is, attracted to persons of both sexes. Thus, some identification with both parents is likely to occur, and it is this identification with parental behaviors and attitudes that sets the stage for the development of the *superego*. In his writings, Freud implied that identification of boys with their fathers during this period was stronger than girls' identification with either parent. This led him to conclude that the superego, or sense of morality, tended to be better developed in males than in females.

During the *latency period* which follows the phallic stage and lasts until puberty, sexual impulses are, for the most part, repressed. They are reactivated during adolescence, and the person enters the *genital stage*. While the sexual instincts during the three early pregenital stages were narcissistic in nature, (i.e., focused on the child's own bodily gratifications) self-love changes into a more genuine, less selfish love for others during this last period of psychosexual development. The sexual instinct becomes directed toward the aim of biological reproduction. This stage, during which the person is expected to become fully socialized (work, marry, raise a family) lasts through adulthood. With extreme old age and senility, the person tends to regress to the pregenital period (Hall, 1954).

In order to progress from one stage of development to the next, Freud hypothesized that the individual must obtain the "right" amount of stimulation appropriate for that period. For example, if a child is to move on from the oral to the anal stage, he must receive from his parents, especially from his mother, some optimal amount of oral gratification; he should be neither deprived nor overindulged. What is "too much" or "too little" gratification is not specified, but Freud did propose two likely consequences of a child's not having received the proper amount of stimulation at a given stage: regression and fixation. If during a given stage—for example, the oral stage— the child obtains insufficient oral stimulation, he is likely to become fixated at that stage; he cannot move "successfully" to the next stage and will probably continue to seek oral gratifications all his life. He will develop what Freud called oral characteristics: that is, he may seek oral gratification by overeating, smoking, or drinking; he may become overly dependent upon others as an infant is dependent on its mother for nourishment, or talk too much, or be verbally aggressive, and so forth. Freud considered characteristics such as extreme tidiness or compulsivity (anal-retentive) and extreme messiness (anal-expulsive) as reflecting fixation at the anal stage of development.

If, during a particular stage, a child is overindulged and given too much gratification, he is likely to exhibit regression. That is, whenever at some later period in life he experiences difficulties and becomes anxious, he is likely to revert to behaviors characteristic of an earlier stage of development—one that was extremely gratifying and not fraught with difficulties or obstacles to satisfaction.

ANXIETY AND PSYCHOLOGICAL DEFENSES

An individual, threatened by potential dangers or withdrawal of satisfactions, experiences fear. These threats to a person's functioning could, according to Freud, have their origins in the environment or in the personality itself. He suggested three kinds of anxiety, each arising from a particular kind of threat or danger. *Reality anxiety* is fear of real danger in the external world, such as fear of being killed or wounded by the enemy in battle. *Neurotic anxiety* is defined as a person's fear that his id instincts will get out of control and cause him to do something for which he will be punished—for example, an adolescent's fear of masturbating, being caught, and being publicly humiliated as a result. *Moral anxiety* refers to a fear of one's conscience, such as fear of having "dirty" or violent fantasies because of the guilt experienced afterwards.

Freud spoke of anxiety as a kind of warning signal which seems to alert the person to impending danger. Once aroused, anxiety impels the person to some sort of action aimed at reducing the anxiety. It is the ego's task to deal with these threats and to somehow relieve the pressure experienced as anxiety. It may accomplish this task by means of realistic, logical solutions and actions, or it may resort to reliance upon *defense mechanisms,* ways of denying or distorting reality and thereby alleviating anxiety, at least temporarily. These defenses operate unconsciously and may take a number of forms. We have already discussed two of these mechanisms, *fixation* and *regression,* which result from anxiety experienced at difficult points in the course of development. Let us go on to define the other major defense mechanisms.

Repression is said to occur when an unacceptable and anxiety-causing instinctual impulse, usually sexual or aggressive in nature, pushes for expression and is forced out of consciousness. Material that has been repressed may express itself by means of displacement. For example, a boy's strong aggressive impulses toward his dominant father may be repressed because of his fear of being punished if he should act upon them. He may redirect the aggressive impulses toward a safer substitute object (his little brother) or may express hostility toward authority figures in general. Another form of displacement discussed by Freud is sublimation, the channeling of unacceptable instinctual desires into socially acceptable activities. Freud felt that human civilization with all its social, artistic, and technological achievements was essentially the result of this sublimation, or rechanneling, of primitive instinctual energies. But displacement in any form never completely reduces tension; expressing repressed urges symbolically is only partially successful.

Projection occurs when a person denies the existence of his own unacceptable thoughts and/or behaviors and attributes them to others. This is another kind of substitutive mechanism. For example, a man might feel envy and hatred toward a co-worker who is a nice, easygoing person and who is very highly skilled at his job. Having no socially acceptable reason for his hostile feelings, the man might "project" them onto his colleague and come to believe that "this man hates me." This projection reduces his anxiety and, at the same time, gives him an excuse for hostile actions toward the person who is now defined as an enemy who has bad intentions.

Another defense involving substitution is reaction formation. A mother who, for example, has feelings of hatred toward her newborn baby whose birth severely curtailed her freedom, might act excessively loving and overprotective toward the child. A person who is made anxious by his own sexual desires might, with extreme self-righteousness, engage in an anti-smut campaign. Both these examples involve a person's substituting in awareness an opposite socially approved desire for one which is anxiety arousing. Reaction formations always involve extreme or excessive behaviors which represent the complete opposite of the unacceptable impulse.

Denial is a fairly primitive defense mechanism that tends to be seen in small children. It involves a kind of magical thinking, in which the person pretends that whatever is causing anxiety does not exist. He pretends that something bad never really happened because he wishes it hadn't.

Rationalization, a very common type of defense, occurs when an individual substitutes a rational or acceptable reason for his own illogical or unacceptable behaviors. A student in the midst of an argument might, for example, rush out of his dorm into a snowstorm without any coat or boots and come back later, soaked through and freezing, with the explanation that he did this as an experiment in withstanding harsh conditions (rather than admitting that this act was just an angry impulse or that he wanted his friends to worry about him).

All of the defense mechanisms represent the ego's attempts to alleviate anxiety. Everyone unconsciously relies upon one or another of these defenses under anxiety-arousing conditions. Overreliance upon these mechanisms, however, is thought to result in serious problems, since all of them involve distortion or denial of reality. Freud felt that if a person relied heavily upon defenses and if, for whatever reason, his defenses failed him, he would become overwhelmed with anxiety and would experience a serious breakdown or collapse (Hall, 1954).

PSYCHOANALYTIC PSYCHOTHERAPY

According to psychoanalytic theory, the three aspects of mental functioning—id, ego, and superego—carry on a kind of constant warfare. The id seeks immediate satisfaction of instinctual (sexual, aggressive) impulses; the superego tries to control those impulses which are not socially approved or permissible; and the ego attempts to adjust the demands of the id and the superego to those of the real world.

The superego reacts not only to unacceptable acts, but also to a person's unacceptable thoughts or desires. It performs its work by repressing or pushing down into the unconscious these unacceptable ideas and impulses. But repressed ideas, according to Freud, will always continue to express themselves; if direct expression of primitive impulses is impossible, then they will find less direct means of manifesting themselves.

Most of the symptoms commonly regarded as maladjusted or pathological are assumed to result from the repression of powerful id impulses. Psychological disorders or symptoms are viewed as either: (1) indirect, symbolic expressions of unconscious impulses; (2) attempts to maintain control of impulses; or (3) both of these. For example, so-called "hysterical" symptoms, physical difficulties with no known organic cause, are seen as "conversions" of unacceptable id impulses into physical symptoms. A young girl with a strong, unconscious desire to get rid of her selfish, invalid mother might develop a paralysis of one or both arms. According to Freudian notions, this symptom might be interpreted as serving both of the functions mentioned above. Her repressed urge to kill her mother and her fear of acting out this wish are *symbolically* expressed through the symptom; she cannot lose control and "strike out" at her mother if her arm is paralyzed. And her paralysis might also render her incapable of taking care of her mother; by reducing this hated burden, her hostility might decrease and she might maintain control of these feelings.

Another example of how psychoanalysts interpret neurotic symptoms involves patients who feel compelled to repeat over and over again certain thoughts (obsessions) or behaviors (compulsions). A person might develop certain counting habits, repeatedly check to see that all doors are locked, wash his hands thirty or forty times every day, and so on. The compulsive hand washing would be viewed as a symbolic expression of sexual impulses repressed by the person's overly strong superego, probably resulting from childhood experiences in a family in which sex was considered "dirty." Fear of germs or contamination masks fear of punishment for acting out sexual desires.

It can be seen from this somewhat oversimplified analysis that Freud saw psychopathology largely as the result of repressed unconscious impulses. It follows from this hypothesis that the major task of psychotherapy is to release these unconscious impulses, to have the person accept them, and to allow them to come under the control of the conscious ego. The sexual and aggressive impulses are regarded as instinctual and, therefore, cannot be eliminated. At the same time, Freud believed it would be impossible to maintain a civilized society in which the instincts could be freely expressed. What Freud proposed as the ideal of good adjustment involved the individual's conscious understanding of his impulses and his adjusting them to the demands of reality.

Freud suggested certain conditions which must be maintained in the psychotherapy situation in order to make it possible for the patient to release or uncover repressed material. Most important is the therapist's attitude; he should be accepting and nonjudgmental. The patient may relax on a couch or an easy chair, and he is encouraged to say whatever comes to mind, without fear of criticism or moralizing on the part of the therapist.

To give both himself and the therapist clues or pathways into his unconscious, the patient is asked to relate dreams, in which unconscious impulses presumably reveal themselves in symbolic ways. The patient talks about the *manifest content* of the dream, what he actually remembers happening in the dream. But the therapist's interest is focused upon the dream's so-called *latent content*, the symbolic meaning of the dream which is thought to represent instinctual id impulses. The patient will also be taught to *free associate*—to let his mind range freely, one association leading to another, without trying to talk about or focus on any particular topic. The therapist may have the patient free associate to certain events or characters that have appeared in his dreams. While the repressed or unconscious material is being uncovered through these methods, the therapist will react with *interpretations*; that is, he will explain or help the patient to arrive at an explanation of his own unconscious thoughts and motivations. Ideally, a learning process takes place and the patient becomes better able to interpret his own behavior and to understand his unconscious motives with less and less guidance from the analyst.

The uncovering of repressed material sometimes leads to dramatic expression of repressed emotional memories, *catharsis*. Recognition of such repressions followed by interpretation leads to *insight*, conscious awareness of one's underlying motives. Making conscious what was unconscious presumably allows the person to deal with his conflicts realistically; the ego becomes strengthened and symptoms may be reduced or eliminated. The psychic energy which is no longer bound in repressed material and defensive behaviors may be released in socially acceptable ways (sublimation).

Freud's observation that his patients seemed to project onto the therapist feelings toward their parents led him to stress the notion of *transference*. At first, since the therapist is permissive and encouraging, the patient experiences a positive transference and is most cooperative. But the patient also "transfers" his negative feelings toward his parents to the therapist; he goes through a long period during which he resists cooperating freely in the therapy procedures. Freud felt that this phenomenon must be understood and explained in terms of the person's childhood experiences and that these must be explored in detail. This process of "working through" the negative transference was thought to be necessary for understanding one's most basic, long-term characteristics.

The psychoanalytic method of treatment has undoubtedly led to many insights about the hidden and not clearly understood aspects of motivation. The treatment, however, is considered suitable only for certain kinds of people. Most often, psychoanalytic clients are relatively affluent (because of the expense of a treatment program which lasts for several years), educated, intelligent, and verbal. In addition, many psychoanalysts recognize that this method is not particularly well suited to the treatment of psychotic patients, psychopaths, or those with below-average intelligence.

Although many new techniques of therapy have been worked out by followers of Freud, as well as by non-Freudians, all psychotherapies which involve talking about problems as a way of gaining insight rely upon one or another of the specific techniques used by Freud: permissive and accepting therapist attitude, transference, catharsis, and interpretation.

REPRESENTATIVE RESEARCH

There exists a vast body of research literature involving attempts to test hypotheses derived from Freud's theory. Many studies are based upon data gathered by clinicians working within the psychoanalytic framework. These reports and interpretations of patients' behaviors and experiences during long-term psychotherapy are examples of the case-study method. Other studies have been done using more objective experimental techniques (larger subject populations, formal personality-assessment instruments, control groups, techniques for reducing experimenter bias, quantitative analyses of data, etc.). There has been, and continues to be, a great deal of disagreement among psychologists regarding the relative acceptability and meaningfulness of data collected by means of case-study versus experimental methods. Many practicing psychoanalysts are prone to discount experimental studies, viewing them as incapable of dealing with Freudian concepts except in a trivial or distorting manner. They suggest, for example, that laboratory studies of "repression" are dealing with a phenomenon that is essentially different from the kind of repression that Freud was concerned with. They claim, too, that it is impossible to study any really important psychological event using the experimental method because, in doing so, one must necessarily ignore or minimize the complex relationships, the dynamics, which characterize psychoanalytic theory. On the other side of the argument are those who contend that the case-study method is a useful observational source for *generating* hypotheses about human behavior, but that it is too subjective to allow for reliable and valid *testing* of hypotheses.

While it is difficult to choose a single experimental study which best represents psychoanalytic research, the following study is one which focuses upon an important construct in the theory, the Oedipus complex, and which uses an interpretive strategy which is quite frequently encountered in research of this kind. Calvin Hall (1963) set out to discover empirical evidence supporting Freud's notions about the Oedipus complex. As described early in this chapter, Freud suggested that boys and girls experience the oedipal period in different ways. That is, their attitudes (loving, hating, fearing) toward their parents follow different courses. The female child's feelings about both parents are more ambivalent than are those of the male child. As Hall states this difference: "She neither fears nor resents the father as much as the boy does, nor does she love and covet the mother as much as he does" (p. 337).

The present study involves the use of dreams, which are viewed by Freudians as an important source of data, a pathway to the unconscious. Using dreams from the files of the Institute of Dream Research, Hall was able to select a sample of dreams collected from people differing in age and sex. The dreamers themselves recorded their dreams on standard report forms which included questions about both the dream and the dreamer. Small children reported their dreams to adults who recorded them. All dreams were analyzed for character and content using standard scoring manuals developed at the Institute of Dream Research.

Hall began the study with two major assumptions: (1) that people dream about persons who are in some way connected with conflicts, anxieties, and frustrations which have their source in early childhood experience, and (2) that, in dreams, any male strangers who appear symbolize the dreamer's father. Hall then formulated the following hypotheses: (1) more strangers in dreams are males than females; (2) there is a higher proportion of male strangers in male dreams than in female dreams; (3) there is a higher proportion of aggressive encounters by the dreamer with male strangers than with female strangers, familiar males, or familiar females; (4) the proportion of aggressive encounters with male strangers is greater for male dreamers than for female dreamers; (5) when subjects are asked to free associate to male strangers who appear in their dreams, they will give more father and male authority-figure associations than any other class of association.

EXERCISE: JUSTIFY HYPOTHESIS ON BASIS OF THEORY.

There were six large groups of subjects, six age groups, used in the study; the dreamers ranged in age from two to eighty years. The results indicate varying degrees of support for the five hypotheses. In all groups but one, there was a higher proportion of male strangers than of female strangers in the reported dreams. The hypothesized higher proportion of male strangers in male dreams than in female dreams was found to be statistically significant in two groups, thus providing only partial support for the hypothesis. There were, as predicted, more aggressive encounters with male strangers than with other dream characters, but these differences were much more prevalent for male than for female groups. The prediction that males were more likely than females to have dreams involving aggressive encounters with male strangers also was partially supported by the data. In two of the six age groups this difference was statistically significant. In two other groups, the difference was in the predicted direction but not significant; and at the two lowest age levels, the difference was in the reverse direction from that predicted. Results dealing with the free association hypothesis provide some support for the prediction, but are based upon data collected from a fairly small sample of subjects and, for this reason, are deemed inconclusive by Hall.

In terms of research strategy, the present study seems to have certain advantages over the less formal case-study method. Hall was able to gather his data from a large sample of subjects at different age levels. The dreams were reported in standard form and scored according to a standard manual, presumably by researchers who did not know the subjects. Using large samples and focusing on specific dream events, Hall was able to subject the data to quantitative analysis. Hypotheses regarding the Oedipus complex were thus tested somewhat more objectively and rigorously in Hall's study than in earlier studies based on psychoanalysts' reports of their patients' dreams.

It is, however, necessary to question the meaning of Hall's investigation on another level and to point to what many see as a pervasive difficulty of psychoanalytic research. Symbolic interpretation of dreams, waking fantasies, or any other kind of material necessarily relies upon essentially untestable assumptions (e.g., the present assumption that male strangers in dreams *always* symbolize the dreamer's father). The problem is that any image or event may be said to symbolize many different things. In the present study, for example, one could come up with a plausible common-sense explanation of Hall's results without referring to Freud's theory at all. Rather than assuming that dream events are symbolic of early childhood attitudes and experiences, one could account for the findings by looking instead at common characteristics of our society. Males, expected and taught to be more outgoing and to get out into the world rather than staying close to home, are perhaps more likely to encounter, or to dream about encountering, a greater number of male strangers than are females. Certainly this seems to be true in books, films, and television shows, where it is almost always the case that the more adventurous male has a greater number of outside contacts, while the female gets out less and her connections with others are more limited in number. It also seems to be generally the case that males are very often involved in competition (athletic, occupational, etc.) with other males, and that winning or coming out on top is very highly valued for men in our society. For males, both competition and aggressive behaviors in the service of competition are socially sanctioned behaviors. And the male who asserts himself, especially in the face of danger or authority, is regarded as manly and heroic. It is not surprising, therefore, that competitive and aggressive relations with males are more prevalent in the dreams of males than in those of females. Obviously, there is no way of demonstrating that this straightforward cultural explanation of the results is better or "more true" than Hall's psychoanalytic explanation, or vice versa. And that is precisely the problem. Relying upon symbolic interpretations as evidence for one's hypotheses is a weak strategy because it is not possible to rule out alternative explanations for one's findings.

MAJOR CONTRIBUTIONS

There can be no doubt that Freud made many extremely important contributions to the understanding of human behavior and that a number of his assumptions, discoveries, and techniques regarding personality and psychotherapy are widely accepted, even by psychologists with nonpsychoanalytic orientations. Many current approaches to psychotherapy still operate on the principle that the expression of and awareness of unconscious motivation and/or feelings is a necessary precondition of improved adjustment. Freud's emphasis on unconscious motivation, the importance of early childhood experiences, the description of defense mechanisms, and the exploration of human sexual motivation all represented major advances in the field.

SUMMARY AND ANALYSIS OF FREUDIAN THEORY

The basic assumptions of Freud's theory are quite clearly stated. The most central assumptions are those dealing with the notion of psychic determinism (all behavior is motivated or goal directed) and the assumption of unconscious psychological processes (the individual is frequently unaware of the motives for his behavior). The third major assumption of the theory is that of instincts. Freud felt that in order to explain motivation or behavior, he had to postulate a physical source of energy which, in some mysterious way, is converted to so-called psychic energy. As a result of the interaction of inherited instinctual energies and the environment, personality tends to be fixed quite early in life. While specific behaviors may change as a result of experience, all major personality variables are thought to remain very stable after the first six years of development.

Extensive change in personality, according to Freud, can take place only as a result of a thorough psychoanalysis (usually of several years' duration). Even with extensive psychoanalytic treatment, most orthodox Freudian analysts see limits to the amount of change possible. The instincts are fixed. Insight into one's expression of unconscious instinctual forces allows for increased ego control and change, but character fixations are considered to be extremely difficult to eradicate. Therapy, as a result, is more often oriented toward the patient's understanding, accepting, and adjusting to his own character structure than it is toward major change.

The dependence of Freudian theory upon instinctual explanations has been the focus of a great deal of criticism. Instinctual drives are presumed to be present, but one cannot predict the strength of these drives on the basis of any known or observable antecedent conditions. Only *after* a person has shown extremely aggressive behavior, for example, can one say that he has strong aggressive instincts; only *post*diction and not *pre*diction, is possible using instinctual notions. Neither may the presence of instincts be measured directly. Instincts may appear without disguise (as in the overtly aggressive person), they may be present but repressed (as in the overly timid or submissive individual), or they may occur in a variety of symbolic forms which require subjective interpretation on the part of the clinician. Because of these difficulties, many contemporary neo-Freudians have abandoned the instinct theory or at least have tended to disregard it in their writings and clinical practice.

In general, Freud's theory is remarkably complete in the network of relationships among its constructs. For example, the defense mechanisms are linked to the energy systems of the three mind entities. The development of the psychosexual instincts through stages is related, in turn, to the development of the id, ego, and superego. If fixation takes place early in the child's life, the ego tends to be weaker. The formation of the superego is dependent upon the satisfactory resolution of the Oedipus complex. All of these relationships, as well as others, are explicit, with the direction of the relationships specified in many instances. The nature of relationships among constructs at higher levels of abstraction, however, tends to be more clearly specified than is the case with lower-level constructs. In dealing with constructs closer to specific behaviors, the direction and nature of the relationships is somewhat confusing or incomplete. Repressed energies are presumed to lead to sublimation, or reaction formation, or symbolic expressions of impulses, and so on. But what is not spelled out is whether this occurs all the time or some of the time, or why one mechanism occurs in one person and a different one in another.

With regard to the ways in which the theory deals with antecedent and consequent conditions, there are both strengths and weaknesses to be found. For many constructs, no clear-cut antecedent conditions are specified. Instincts, the Oedipus complex, and castration fears, are treated as givens. For other constructs, such as oral fixation and failure to resolve the Oedipus complex, antecedents are described. But, in many cases, the antecedent conditions are presented in a way which is not particularly useful. For example, the antecedents for oral fixation are either too little gratification during the oral stage, too much gratification, inconsistent gratification, or traumatic weaning experiences. These conditions are not carefully described — it is not clear what the "right" amount of stimulation is — and, on a post hoc basis, the descriptions could be applied to almost anyone. This same criticism can be applied to mechanisms that lie at the heart of psychoanalysis. The theory states that if the superego is strong, repression will occur. But it does not attempt to answer the question of where repression comes from. It is simply assumed that such behavior is inborn.

Despite these weaknesses, however, there are many instances in which the theory specifies connections between observations, intermediate and higher-order constructs. In this sense, the theory is a "rich" one; that is, it allows one to generate, from relatively little data, a large number of hypotheses about an individual.

Classical psychoanalysis presents many constructs which, by their very nature, are difficult to operationalize. This is due to the fact that much of the theory deals with assumed unconscious processes which the individual cannot describe or report directly, and with unconscious drives which are rarely expressed in a direct fashion. How can you tell if a person is repressing something if, in fact, this repression can lead to many different kinds of expressed behavior? How does one know if an instinctive force is weak or strong? If someone likes to paint, is this an

activity that is satisfying for its own sake or does it represent the sublimation of sexual instincts? Is the smoking of a pipe evidence of oral fixation or simply the result of some socialization process? Is a sloppy desk
the result of too much work or of anal fixation? Does the tendency to
overindulge a child reflect, on the part of the mother, a strong love for
her offspring, or is it a reaction formation to an unconscious rejection of
motherhood?

In Freud's theory, a certain behavior or phenomenon may be the result
of a number of different antecedent experiences. Similarly, a particular
experience during childhood may lead to a number of possible behaviors
or response patterns later in life. Because the antecedents and/or consequences for a given construct are often numerous and not clearly defined, it is extremely difficult to arrive at operations which are generally
agreed upon as adequate for measuring a construct, or for testing the relationship between two constructs. Frequently, operations which would
be widely accepted as meaningful are those which cannot be manipulat-
ed experimentally, such as a weaning trauma or a rejecting, punitive
father. Consequently, the operations used in experimental studies are
often rejected by psychoanalytic practitioners as superficial and not sufficiently related to the theory (Rapaport, 1959). The operational problem
is further complicated by the theory's reliance upon symbolism which
gives one a great deal of freedom of interpretation.

One of the reasons why psychoanalysis has such great appeal to clinicians is that it provides both a process and a content theory. The process
theory is necessary for deriving psychotherapeutic procedures, while the
content theory is used to characterize individual differences. Both the
process and content variables range broadly from general to specific.
Freud's theory is indeed rich in content variables. People are said to differ in the amount of instinctual drive, in the strengths of the competing
internal forces of id, ego, and superego, in the kinds of defenses they rely
upon, in their choice of sexual objects, and in the traits which characterize fixations at different stages of psychosexual development. While
Freud was not always clear in his description of these variables, he illus-
trated them in numerous published case studies.

For Freud, the dynamics of personality are internal dynamics. The instinctual drives and the interaction of the id, ego, and superego are the
major determinants of behavior. At the same time, Freud does make dis-
tinctions between certain kinds of situational variables. For example, he
refers not infrequently to sex and authority relationships, and he specifies in his case studies how individuals respond differently to males ver-

sus females, or to authority figures versus people not representing authority. At least to this extent, situational variables play a role in Freud's behavioral predictions.

In summary, Freud presented a complex theory that attempted to explain the deeper, unconscious life of the person. It has been rich as a source of hypotheses for psychology but has lacked scientific rigor. Freud's dependence upon instinct formulations and the tremendous importance he attached to sex as a source of motivation have been strongly criticized by subsequent theorists. While the theory itself has many problems, it has led to a kind of in-depth study of individuals that has resulting in many provocative observations.

What is important for the modern student of personality is not whether Freud was right or wrong in all he said, but rather, how to state his many insights into human nature in ways that can be objectively confirmed or rejected.

4

Erikson's Psychosocial Theory of Development

Erik Erikson (1963; 1964; 1968) is a contemporary ego psychologist whose theory represents an attempt to extend and build upon the foundations of Freud's psychoanalytic theory. Like other so-called neo-Freudians (e.g., Fromm, Horney, Sullivan), Erikson emphasizes the importance of ego functions and social influences in attempts to understand personality. Erikson is best known for his theory of psychosocial development, which he views as an extension of Freud's ideas concerning the individual's progression through a series of psychosexual stages. Unlike Freud, however, Erikson focuses a great deal of attention on both the latency period (middle childhood) and adolescence. Indeed, his developmental stages extend from infancy through adulthood into old age.

EIGHT AGES OF MAN: THE PSYCHOSOCIAL STAGES

Erikson describes the human life cycle in terms of a series of stages through which the individual passes. Each stage is characterized by an important crisis, or turning point, in the development of personality. He assumes that there are certain inner laws of development and that, given a reasonable amount of proper guidance, the child will pass through each crisis successfully "with an increased sense of inner unity, with an increase of good judgment, and an increase in the capacity to do well according to his own standards and the standards of those who are significant to him" (1968, p. 92). The crises are described as a series of alternative basic attitudes — for example, basic trust versus basic mistrust, autonomy versus shame and doubt, and so on. The basic attitude which develops most strongly during a particular stage depends upon the quality of the individual's interpersonal experiences during that stage of development. Erikson points out that although a particular conflict or crisis is dominant during each individual stage, development is a continuous process. Therefore, all of the conflicts are present in some form throughout one's lifetime, and current conflicts are influenced by the person's experiences during earlier psychosocial stages.

Basic Trust Versus Basic Mistrust

The relationship with the mother or caretaker during early infancy is as important for Erikson as it was for Freud. The basic attitudes of trust versus mistrust begin to develop during this period of early infancy. Erikson's use of the term trust implies an essential trust in others and a basic sense of one's own trustworthiness. This trusting attitude is viewed as the cornerstone of a healthy personality, and it evolves out of the mutual regulation which develops between mother and child. Erikson emphasizes that it is the quality of the maternal relationship which is important, rather than the quantity of love or of oral satisfactions which the mother provides. When the mother's caretaking involves sensitivity to the needs of the infant and when the mother can be relied upon to be consistent in her care, the child feels secure. Without such proper care and guidance, the child is likely to develop an attitude of basic mistrust and feelings of estrangement and anxiety. Such an attitude characterizes people who, later in life, tend to withdraw into themselves whenever difficulties arise.

Autonomy Versus Shame and Doubt

Just as the first psychosocial stage coincides with Freud's oral stage, this second stage in Erikson's theory parallels in time the anal period of development. It is during this period that the child experiments with two sets of social modalities: "holding on" and "letting go." It is the child's task to learn how to alternate these patterns appropriately, in accordance with society's conventions. The toilet-training period often represents a battle for autonomy; when the training is not properly handled, the child may regress to behaviors characteristic of the oral stage or may become hostile and willful. The controls exercised by parents at this time must be firm and reassuring, so that the child can gain a sense of self-control without experiencing a great deal of shame and doubt. He must learn how to cooperate without losing his self-esteem. If he experiences frequent losses of self-control or if his parents react to accidents with attempts to overcontrol the child, he will develop strong feelings of shame and doubt. If, on the other hand, training progresses smoothly, the child develops a budding sense of autonomy, good will, and pride. These contrasting attitudes (autonomy versus shame and doubt) are important in terms of later personality development. The stage of autonomy represents the first emancipation and influences the individual's later attempts at further emancipation during the adolescent years. Erikson suggests that the development of trust is necessary for the growth of autonomy; if the child begins this stage mistrusting others and himself, he is likely to experience difficulty.

Initiative Versus Guilt

This third psychosocial stage coincides with Freud's phallic stage of development. It is characterized by a great deal of exploratory behavior and curiosity about sexual matters. The basic modality during this period involves "being on the make," which Erikson describes as enjoyment of competition and conquest. During this stage, the child ideally resolves his oedipal conflicts by identifying with the parent and learning what the limits on initiative are. The child's conscience develops during this period and the beginnings of the process of self-judgment appear. In addition, he learns what is possible and what kinds of goals are desirable. Erikson points out that at this point in time the individual begins to be "forever divided in himself." That is, he is part child and part parent as soon as he starts to engage in self-observation, self-guidance, and self-punishment. Successful resolution of the basic conflict at this stage results in the child's developing a healthy sense of iniative, coupled with the establishment of a good moral sense. Difficulties at this stage may lead to problems such as loss of initiative, fearfulness, and excessive feelings of guilt.

Industry Versus Inferiority

Unlike Freud, Erikson stresses the importance of the latency period, during which the child learns to win recognition by producing things.

Sooner or later, children become dissatisfied with games and make-believe and begin to develop what Erikson refers to as a sense of industry. Although violent drives (id drives) are normally dormant during this period, this is a very decisive stage in terms of social development.

In all cultures, children at this stage receive some form of systematic instruction, such as formal schooling, apprenticeship, and so on. The child develops positive identifications with people who know how to do things which are valued by society, and he begins to develop rudimentary technological skills. In addition, the child must learn how to work with others in order to produce things successfully. If he is not good at doing things, if he becomes discouraged by competing with his peers in important skill areas, he may develop strong feelings of inadequacy or inferiority. This is most likely to occur if the child's family life has failed to prepare him adequately for school life, or if his school experiences are unpleasant and nonsupportive. Successful resolution of conflicts at this stage leads to a healthy sense of industry, feelings of self-confidence, and developing feelings of identity as a potentially useful and productive person in society.

Identity Versus Role Confusion

Erikson speaks of adolescence as a period of uprootedness in human life. "Like a trapeze artist, the young person in the middle of vigorous motion must let go of his safe hold on childhood and reach out for a firm grasp on adulthood, depending for a breathless interval on a relatedness between the past and the future, and on the reliability of those he must let go of, and those who will 'receive' him" (1964, p. 90). During this most crucial period, young people are most concerned with what they appear to be in the eyes of others as compared with what they feel they are, and with the problem of how to match their skills with the occupational roles available to them in the culture. The establishment of a healthy *ego identity* represents the major task of this period. Erikson often describes adolescence as a psychosocial moratorium, a period during which the young adult may experiment with various roles in the hopes of finding a niche for himself in society. Adult commitments are delayed; society is somewhat permissive and allows the young person some time to "find himself." During this moratorium, young people experiment with a variety of roles and behaviors. For some, it is a time of self-sacrifice and involvement in idealistic causes; others spend this period immersed in academic pursuits, engaged in youthful pranks or out-right delinquency, traveling, seeking psychological or psychiatric treat-ment, and so on.

Through childhood, the individual experiences a succession of tenta-tive identities, so that he feels that he knows who and what he is. But discontinuities in development cause the sense of identity to change again and again — the "little boy" must now act like a "big boy" and then like a "real man." It is the task of the ego to bridge these discontinuities between different levels of personality development. Successful resolu-tion of the conflicts of adolescence results in the development of a healthy sense of identity; the person feels comfortable with his body, feels that he knows who he is and where he is going, and feels confident that others will recognize his worth.

The danger of this stage is *identity confusion.* In most instances, this is the result of an inability to settle on an occupational identity. In other cases, confusion may be based on strong previous doubts concerning one's sexual identity. A certain amount of confusion or "diffusion" at this stage is normal, for the young adult is experimenting with a variety of roles and values and attitudes toward the world. Many adolescents overidentify with cliques and culture heroes. Often, young people "fall in love" for the first time. Erikson points out that falling in love during this stage is usually not entirely, or even primarily, a sexual matter. Rather, adolescent love is "an attempt to arrive at a definition of one's identity by projecting one's diffused ego image on another and seeing it thus reflected and gradually clarified. This is why so much of young love is conversation" (1968, p. 132). He also stresses that young adoles-cents are often extremely cliquish and are often cruel in excluding from their in-groups persons who are "different" or "out of it." This intoler-ance of differences is viewed as a defense against a sense of identity loss. Young people help each other and bolster their identity by banding to-gether and stereotyping themselves, their ideals, their enemies, their ways of speaking and dressing, and so on.

Some adolescents and young adults suffer from more serious identity confusion. They cannot hold up under the simultaneous pressures of committing themselves to some occupational choice, of difficult compe-tition, of self-definition, and of establishing intimate relations with others. Any latent weaknesses as a result of difficulties experienced dur-ing earlier psychosocial stages are likely to be revealed by such pres-sures. The symptoms of severe identity confusion include a painful sense of isolation, a loss of initiative, and an inability to concentrate on tasks (or, at the other extreme, complete preoccupation with one kind of activity). In addition, the individual may display scornful and snobbish hostility toward the roles which are suggested as desirable and proper by his family or community. This scornful attitude may take the form of rejection of one's social class, sex role, ethnic background, a dislike for everything American, and so on. Often, severe identity confusion leads to the choice of a *negative identity*, that is, an identity which is clearly seen as undesirable, disgusting, or dangerous by one's family. Sometimes, an adolescent would rather be very crazy or very bad of his own choice than be "ordinary" or feel like a nobody.

Intimacy Versus Isolation

It is only when identity formation is well on its way that genuine intimacy is possible. Erikson defines true intimacy as a stable commitment to another person and an ability to abide by such a strong commitment, which may involve personal sacrifices and compromises. The young adult who is not sure of his identity either shies away from intimate relationships or engages in a kind of promiscuous intimacy without real commitment.

The counterpart of intimacy is distantiation, "the readiness to isolate and, if necessary, destroy those forces and people whose essence seems dangerous to one's own" (1968, p. 136). Thus, the danger of this stage is isolation; when this occurs, the individual avoids contacts which commit him to intimacy. His relations with others may become very stereotyped, shallow, and nonrewarding.

Generativity Versus Stagnation

The mature adult needs to be needed. Erikson's concept of generativity refers to the concern for establishing and guiding the next generation. This concern may be expressed in different ways by different people. For some, it is expressed through raising a family. For others who, for whatever reason, have no family of their own, productivity and creativity which represent a useful contribution to society is a way of expressing concern for the next generation. Generativity involves the expansion of one's ego interest to include others. When this does not develop, the individual often experiences a sense of stagnation, boredom, and interpersonal impoverishment. Very often, too, stagnation of this kind leads people to regressive behavior. Specifically, it leads them to indulge themselves as if they were their own or one another's one and only child. They focus too much attention on themselves and on their own physical and psychological difficulties.

Ego Integrity Versus Despair

Erikson describes ego integrity as the fruit of the seven earlier developmental stages of the life cycle. While this concept is not easily defined, it seems to refer to an acceptance of one's life cycle and of the people who have become significant to it as, in some sense, inevitable. One can thus accept and love one's parents without wishing that they had been different. It also involves accepting the fact that one's life is one's own responsibility, and feeling a sense of comradeship for people of distant times and places and the truths which they have passed down through the ages.

When ego integrity has failed to develop, the individual experiences feelings of despair. He regrets that he cannot start all over again and live his life differently, and death is strongly feared rather than accepted gracefully. Such despair is often masked by attitudes of disgust or misanthropy; the person indirectly expresses contempt for himself by expressing constant displeasure with people or institutions.

REPRESENTATIVE RESEARCH

Erikson's writings include a great deal of case history material by means of which he attempts to show how the development of an individual's personality is shaped by the particular nature of his society or subculture. He has also published several books in which he applied psychological methods in the study of important historical figures, such as Martin Luther and Gandhi.

MAJOR CONTRIBUTIONS

Along with other neo-Freudians, Erikson deemphasized biological determinants while stressing the importance of social influences on the development of personality. Without specifically denying Freud's notions concerning the importance of primitive id impulses, he attempted to build upon psychoanalytic theory by paying particular attention to the reality-oriented and integrative functions of the ego and giving them greater significance in personality development.

Perhaps Erikson's most important contribution involves his extension of the psychoanalytic theory of development to include both the latency period and adolescence. His notions about the importance of ego identity have been quite influential and have stimulated research in the area of identity problems among adolescents in this culture and in other societies. Contemporary psychologists, psychiatrists, and sociologists have used some of Erikson's ideas in their attempts to understand such problems as juvenile delinquency, adolescent depression and psychosis, and student protests.

Although Erikson very explicitly embraces Freudian theory and explains his own theory as an attempt to elaborate Freud's ideas rather than to contradict them, it is clear that Erikson is primarily concerned, as Freud was not, with social and cultural influences on the individual. Since Erikson does not present a full theory of personality but rather an extension and partial revision of Freud's theories, a separate analysis and summary of Erikson's contributions will not be presented.

5

Adler's "Individual Psychology"

An early colleague of Freud's, Alfred Adler (1924) later severed his connection with Freudian psychoanalysis and founded his own school of thought, which he referred to as "Individual Psychology." Although often classified as one of the psychoanalytic school, Adler disagreed with Freud on a number of important issues. He has made his own mark on our society not only in terms of his influence on more recent approaches to personality and psychotherapy, but also on the fields of education and child development.

Adler retained Freud's notion that all behavior is motivated or directed toward some goal. He also recognized that the individual is frequently unaware of his own motivations and often fails to see the meaning or significance of his own behavior. Unlike Freud, however, Adler did not divide the mind into a conscious and an unconscious, nor did he speak of instinctual energy systems. Adler's break with Freud was primarily based upon his disagreement with Freudian instinct theory and Freud's emphasis upon the overriding importance of sexual motivation in the behavior of both children and adults.

As a physician, Adler had studied the processes of physical compensation. He observed that when organisms (animals and human beings) suffered from physical deficiencies—weak or defective organs or bodily parts—they tended to make up or compensate for these deficiencies in one of two ways. In some cases, an organism would show strong development of another organ to take over some or all of the functions of the weak organ (compensation). In other instances, an initially inadequate part of the body would become more than normally strong or effective (overcompensation). Adler regarded these compensatory processes as built-in biological characteristics of living organisms, and this led him to suggest a *psychological* theory of compensation.

THREE MAJOR ASSUMPTIONS

There are three assumptions which, for Adler, provide the motivational basis for essentially all human behavior. These refer to an individual's *feelings of inferiority, striving for superiority,* and *social interest.*

Human infants experience a very long period of dependency, during which they are quite helpless and must depend upon adults to survive. Adler asserted that because the child is so helpless, weak, and dependent upon others, he develops *feelings of inferiority* or *inadequacy.* He believed, also, that it is characteristic of human beings (and of nonhuman organisms as well) to make up for their weaknesses—that is, to compensate and/or overcompensate for deficiencies. Since everyone feels inadequate and dependent upon others early in life, every person attempts to compensate for inferiority by striving for superiority. This *striving for superiority* refers to an individual's attempts to control his environment, to achieve power or strength and thereby make up for perceived weaknesses.

In his later writings, Adler added to his theory another major assumption which he referred to as *social interest* (Adler, 1939). Social interest was defined as a feeling for others, a motive to contribute to society. All human beings were considered to be capable of such social feeling, but certain kinds of experiences could interfere with the development of social interest. The maladjusted person, whose compensatory striving for superiority is overly strong, usually acts in terms of self-interest rather than social interest.

INDIVIDUAL DIFFERENCES

Adler suggested that each person learns from his own immediate environment what constitutes superiority in that setting. Families differ in the kinds of attitudes and behaviors they value most highly. In some families, academic achievement is considered important and a child finds that doing well in school results in parental attention, recognition, and other such rewards. In other families, athletic achievement, aggressiveness, compliant behavior, or social skills tend to be rewarded with attention. According to Adler's theory, each person develops a style of life which is based on or determined by the alternatives for achieving superiority that are offered by his immediate environment.

Individuals may differ from each other in several ways. First, people differ in the degree of inferiority feelings they experience, with some persons suffering from greater feelings of inadequacy than others. Depending upon the attitudes of significant adults, a child who has some physical defect, is a slow learner, is small for his age, and so on, might begin life at a greater disadvantage than a child without such problems. In any case, an individual with very strong feelings of inadequacy is likely to strive harder than do others to overcome or compensate for these feelings.

Second, people differ in their areas of perceived inferiority—such as in physical, intellectual, or social skills. A child who is poor at sports and feels inferior to his playmates in this respect often tries to compensate for this, for example, by means of scholastic achievement. Or, he may attempt to overcompensate, that is, to work intensively at developing athletic skills. The "90-pound weakling," who lifts weights and transforms himself into a "muscle man" so that bullies will no longer kick sand in his face, is a good example of what Adler means by overcompensation.

A third way in which individuals differ involves the style of life they adopt to overcome their feelings of inferiority. They may, as in the examples just discussed, choose to strive for superiority or competence in ways which are considered adaptive or admirable by other people. But, it is sometimes the case that people develop what Adler called a "mistaken style of life," based on early experiences within the family. The child who compensates for his lack of athletic ability by doing well in school work, musical or artistic activities, and so on, has chosen a life style that is likely to be both acceptable and rewarding in future years. On the other hand, the child who sees no such avenues of achievement available to him may try to compensate by striving for attention and recognition in ways which are not at all adaptive. He may strive for superiority by trying to control others by physical strength, by constant clowning, by being very critical and trying to make others look bad, or by peculiar symptoms that have a special symbolic meaning only to him. While such behaviors may be somewhat successful at first in gaining for the child the attention he craves, in the long run they are likely to lead to serious problems and poor relationships with other people.

For Adler, the development of a neurotic or maladjusted style of life was always based upon a child's mistaken perceptions of the world. A child may hear his parents' constant quarreling, observe that the one who shouts loudest and longest wins the arguments, and come to believe that he must argue and fight for everything until he gets what he wants. Another child, feeling rejected by his parents in favor of a younger sibling, may discover that whenever he gets sick his parents once again give him all the attention and love he received before the younger child arrived. As a result, he may develop many physical complaints and become a "delicate child." Seeing the world from their own unique positions, the children described here have developed distorted life styles or patterns of behavior. Once a given style of life has developed, it is difficult to learn from new experiences because these tend to be interpreted along familiar lines—the style of life "screens" new experiences—and the distortion is likely to be maintained.

FAMILY DYNAMICS

Adler objected to Freud's almost exclusive emphasis on the role of parents' behavior in determining the personality and adjustment of the child. While parent-child relationships were regarded by Adler as extremely important developmental influences, his theory also considers in detail the effects of sibling rivalry, family size, and the child's ordinal position.

Parent-Child Relationships

If a child's relationship with his parents is faulty—if it does not provide him with a realistic view of the world that exists beyond the family situation—the child is likely to develop a mistaken style of life. Adler specified two kinds of faulty parent-child relationships: those which involve pampering and those which involve rejection.

The term pampering may refer to several different but overlapping categories of parental behaviors. First, it may involve overprotection; the parents may be fearful about letting the child take even small risks or try out certain activities. Second, pampering may involve overindulgence; in trying to make their son or daughter happy and contented, parents may give in to the child's every whim. And last, pampering may take the form of overdomination; parents who are overly anxious may refuse to allow their child to make any decisions for himself. All of these pampering behaviors tend to make the child feel inadequate and interfere with the development of independence and responsibility.

Pampered children are likely to experience difficulties during the course of growing up. Such children develop an expectation, early in life, that they will always be taken care of by others and that their wishes will be fulfilled. And because they are overprotected and given little responsibility, pampered children need not learn ways of adjusting to real-life situations. Children who are not pampered are in a better position to learn how to cooperate and share with others, how to plan ahead, take the initiative in certain situations, and so on. And when they get out of the protected atmosphere of the home, they are less likely to feel threatened and inadequate. Pampered children have fewer experiences which would make it necessary for them to develop such skills. Instead, they are likely to learn ways of controlling or manipulating other people so that these others will continue to protect and take care of them. Adler felt that pampered children were likely to develop into egocentric and selfish individuals with serious problems in maintaining mutually rewarding relationships with others.

Adler believed that the rejected child is also likely to experience difficulties later in life. Such a child may be unwanted for a variety of reasons: because there are already more children than the parents can afford, because the parents' marital relationship is an unhappy one, because the child is sickly or in some way defective, because the parents did not want any children in the first place, and so on. In terms of actual behaviors, rejection may take several different forms. The child may be treated with hostility or brutality, or the rejection may be more subtle — he may be more or less ignored, left on his own much of the time, or neglected by his parents in favor of a preferred sibling. Whatever the cause of rejection and whatever particular form it takes, the child experiences the world as hostile and/or neglectful. As a result, Adler believed, the child is likely to develop the attitude that people are against him and cannot be relied upon, that he must constantly be on the alert for possible betrayal and must fight for what he wants in life. While the rejected child tends to become independent at an early age, his distrust of people is likely to result in poor interpersonal relationships and little sense of responsibility toward other people or the society in which he lives. According to Adler, the pampered child might be expected to become neurotic, while the rejected child's experience might provide a psychological basis for delinquency and criminal behavior.

Sibling Relationships

Adler considered the child's relationships with his brothers and/or sisters to be important in themselves and important because of their effects on the parent-child relationship. He suggested that as a result of his *ordinal position* in the family (only child, firstborn, middle or youngest child), each child is subjected to special pressures and opportunities.

The only child, according to Adler, holds a very special position. He or she is likely to receive a great deal of parental attention and concern. Only children are frequently pampered by their parents. When this is the case, the child tends to become egocentric and demanding. Overprotected by his family, he may get along well until he goes to school; but he often encounters frustration and difficulties in adjusting to the school environment in which he is not the center of attention.

The oldest child in the family is in an interesting position. His early history may include some sort of pampering and overprotection, since parents are often somewhat anxious the first time around and concerned about doing all the "right" things for their child. Eventually, the oldest child is displaced as the center of attention by the second child. Adler sometimes referred to the firstborn as the "king dethroned," and noted that this might be a very upsetting experience. Seeing that his younger sibling is winning the contest for parental attention, the oldest child may for a while show infantile or destructive behaviors in an effort to regain some of the attention he has lost. Adler suggested that, as he grows up, the oldest child often tends to be accepting of and closely identified with his parents' values. Since he often is given responsibility for (and authority over) his younger brothers and sisters, it makes sense for him to adopt the parents' values and standards.

The middle child in the family is said to enjoy a good position in terms of family pressures and opportunities for learning social skills. Since he has never had an exclusive claim on his parents' attention—he has always had to "share" them with at least one older sibling—his displacement by the next child is not likely to involve too dramatic a change. Since he has siblings from the beginning, he, of necessity, tends to learn social skills (such as cooperation and compromise). He may, however, wish to overthrow the authority of the oldest child; when this is the case, according to Adler, the middle child is likely to grow up with radical notions which differ from those of the parents and the oldest sibling.

The position of the youngest child may be special for several reasons. He may, as the "baby" of the family, be pampered not only by the parents but, especially in large families, by older siblings as well. Or, if his parents are economically burdened, he may hold the position of the "tag-along" kid who has nothing of his own and must get by on hand-me-downs from other family members. In either case, the youngest child occupies a unique position in that he has several competitors in the family, all of whom are bigger and stronger and more privileged than he. Adler sometimes spoke of the "fighting youngest child" as the child most likely to become a revolutionary.

Each of the above examples represents a stereotype, a general description of the "typical" only, oldest, middle, and youngest child. Clearly, not every child in each of these categories will fit the general descriptions proposed by Adler. What is important in terms of understanding the theory is that each child's position in his family is likely to present him with certain kinds of problems—having to give up being the center of attention after having held the spotlight for some time, having to get along with others who have more power than he, and so on. Thus, in discussing the dynamics of the family, Adler's interest was in trying to discover the kinds of problems faced by individuals and the kinds of characteristic solutions people might develop in trying to solve these problems.

MALADJUSTMENT

According to Adler, everyone experiences feelings of inadequacy or inferiority and attempts to compensate for these feelings—that is, strives for superiority. In doing so, each person encounters obstacles to success, problems which need to be solved in order to reach particular goals. Adler introduced several constructs which he found useful in distinguishing between the "normal" person and the maladjusted person in terms of the way each of these deals with problems.

The normal or well-adjusted person approaches problems realistically. In Adler's terms, he shows *courage;* that is, he is not so afraid of failure that he shies away from the truth about himself and the difficult situations he faces. He shows *common sense* and tends to see things as they really are. Third, the well-adjusted person is one who exhibits *social interest*, as opposed to exclusive self-interest; he is concerned about others and wishes to pull his own weight and contribute to society, rather than merely struggling for individual power or success. Adler believed that these characteristics—courage, common sense, and social interest—were innate human potentials which would develop naturally unless they were thwarted. If the striving for superiority is too strong a motive for an individual (because of severe feelings of inferiority or a mistaken view of life), this interferes with the normal development of social interest. All maladjustment, according to Adler, is characterized by lack of social interest (and a preoccupation with self-interest and self-protection).

In developing this concept of social interest, Adler clearly anticipated later writers with similar notions. Thus, for Harry Stack Sullivan, the path to adjustment lay in the direction of developing "the capacity for genuine, unselfish love for others," for Erich Fromm it was "brotherly love," and for A. H. Mowrer, it was accepting "one's social responsibility."

The maladjusted person, when encountering difficulties, tends to turn away from realistic, constructive efforts to solve his problems. In his struggle for superiority, he cannot tolerate failure, he *distances* himself from that failure. He may, for example, spend time daydreaming his problems away. He may find excuses (illness, other problems at home) for doing poorly in his schoolwork or at his job. Or he may develop any of a variety of symptoms which serve to draw attention away from his real problems. Adler used the term *distance* (or *distancing mechanisms*) to include any kind of defensive behavior used by people to protect themselves psychologically from failure and from recognizing painful truths about themselves.

Adler differed sharply from Freud in the way in which he viewed problems in sexual behavior and sex-role behavior. While Freud saw all sexual difficulties as the result of a clash between the individual's instinctual energies and society's repressive influence, Adler believed that sexual problems, like other interpersonal problems, were outcomes of the struggle for power or superiority. Sexuality, in Adler's theory, was not given a central position; it was considered to be one of many important human behaviors. But Adler did introduce two new terms, *masculine protest* and *feminine protest*, in describing certain kinds of sex-role problems.

It was clear to Adler that in many cultures, and in many families, males were dominant; that is, boys were given more privileges, more freedom, more recognition, and higher status than girls. In such societies and in male-dominated families, superiority was seen as related to so-called masculine characteristics: physical strength, assertiveness, and so on. Adler believed that some proportion of girls growing up in this kind of environment came to view the goal of superiority as the goal of becoming more masculine. Suffering from an extra burden of inferiority feelings because they were not male, some females seemed to develop a masculine protest and tried to behave as much like males as they could. As they grew up, such women would perceive men as rivals rather than as partners in a cooperative marital relationship.

Adler recognized that, in a male-dominated culture, men as well as some women strive for masculinity. Boys, too, feel that in order to be accepted and recognized they must become strong, successful, sexually adequate, and so on. Feeling inadequate, some boys—little boys in a world of powerful men—developed styles of life oriented around this striving for masculinity and power. Men whose activities and ways of doing things seem designed to convince themselves and others of their masculinity (e.g., the "machismo" cults and motorcycle toughs) would be seen by Adler as males showing a masculine protest. If these men set their standards for masculine behavior excessively high—so high that they can never convince themselves that they are sufficiently manly—sexual difficulties may develop.

In certain families and subcultures, those with very dominant mother figures or those composed mostly of females, power may be seen as associated with certain "feminine" traits or characteristics. In this kind of environment, according to Adler, children may strive to become extremely "feminine" (e.g., nurturant, motherly, girlish in appearance or gestures, etc.). Either boys or girls might, upon seeing the pathway to superiority as one involving excessive femininity, develop this attitude of feminine protest. Adler believed that a variety of sexual problems—shyness with or fear of members of the opposite sex, sexual unresponsiveness, deviate sexual patterns, and so on—might stem from extreme forms of masculine or feminine protest.

ADLERIAN PSYCHOTHERAPY

Adlerian psychotherapists differ from Freudians in several respects. Although, like psychoanalysts, they explore with the patient his early childhood experiences, they do not rely upon free association and dream interpretation techniques for doing so. They tend to ask more direct questions and to focus upon different kinds of material: early experiences related to sibling rivalry, pampering or rejection by parents, attitudes toward the social roles of males and females, possible failures in learning cooperation and independence, lack of self-confidence, and so on. The psychotherapist's assumption is that the patient's current difficulties stem from these early experiences and from the mistaken style of life developed during childhood. The first step in Adlerian psychotherapy involves the therapist's attempt to discover the individual's style of life.

The second step in this kind of therapy has as its goal the reduction of the patient's feelings of inferiority. Adler saw most neurotic patients as lacking in courage. In their struggle for superiority, they were afraid to fail, and their symptoms were actually defenses against failure. To overcome some of these feelings of inferiority and fear of facing up to problems, Adlerians use direct encouragement and reassurance. Since Adler believed that most patients were so preoccupied with their own problems and needs that they were not sufficiently aware of others' needs, the third step in psychotherapy of this sort involves the therapist's attempts to build social interest on the part of the patient. Independence and cooperative behaviors are actively encouraged, while dependency and exclusive self-interest are discouraged.

In the treatment of children experiencing psychological difficulties, Adler believed that changing and reeducating parents and teachers was of great importance. Pampering or rejecting parents were told that their behaviors were the source of their children's problems, and they were given direct suggestions about new ways of dealing with the children. With both parents and teachers, Adler stressed the child's need for independence and recognition; it was his belief that every child should have his own claim to distinction. It was the job of adults to discover what activities the child was best at and then to encourage and praise the child in those areas. This was seen as a necessary step in reducing feelings of inadequacy and thereby reducing the child's need to engage in destructive or maladaptive behaviors in his effort to obtain attention and recognition. Also emphasized was the need for teaching the child cooperation early in life to encourage the development of social interest. In addition to providing these specific behavioral prescriptions for significant adults in the child's environment, Adler would often see the child directly for treatment purposes. But his meetings with children tended to be brief and were generally designed only to encourage and support them in new and more constructive behaviors. Adler, much like modern behavior therapists, believed that the best way to change a child's behavior was to change factors in the home and school situations which were serving to maintain problem attitudes and behavior.

In the treatment of both adult and child patients, the emphasis upon straightforward, rational discussion and a common-sense approach to solving problems distinguishes Adlerian psychotherapy from Freudian psychoanalysis. Adlerians tend to interpret problems earlier in therapy and to be more directive in terms of suggesting specific changes and courses of action. Since this kind of therapy is more straightforward and relies heavily upon reason or common sense (as compared with long-term exploration of unconscious material), this approach takes less time than Freudian methods.

REPRESENTATIVE RESEARCH

Most of the constructs in Adler's theory have not been studied by means of modern experimental research methods. There does exist, however, a large research literature dealing with the effects of ordinal position upon the development of certain kinds of behaviors. It is not our purpose here to review the literature on ordinal position, but it might be worthwhile to describe in detail one study which investigates the relationship between ordinal position and people's tendency to affiliate with others under stressful circumstances. While the notion that ordinal position is an important variable in personality development derives from Adler's work, many of the more recent studies done in this area have been designed by experimental social psychologists.

In his earliest investigation of the affiliation motive, Stanley Schachter (1959) was interested in studying the relationship between fear and affiliative behavior. Noting that people who were isolated (in shipwrecks, in accidents, as volunteers in experimental studies on the effects of isolation, etc.) often became fearful, Schachter reasoned that affiliation with others might reduce fear; and being in a fear-arousing situation might cause people to wish to affiliate with others. Specifically, Schachter hypothesized that highly fearful persons would show affiliative tendencies significantly more than less fearful people. This hypothesis was tested in a laboratory experiment using the following procedure.

College student subjects were told that they were to participate in an experiment concerning the effects of electric shock. The laboratory room contained several kinds of electrical equipment and the experimenter, who wore a white laboratory coat, introduced himself as a member of the department of neurology and psychiatry. Each subject was given a description of the experiment, and the instructions were designed to arouse either a considerable degree of fear (high-fear condition) or a lesser degree of fear (low-fear condition).

In the high-fear condition, subjects were told that the electric shocks would be quite painful, but would produce no permanent tissue damage. In the low-fear condition, subjects were told that they would receive shocks, but that they would not be painful—only somewhat unpleasant tingling sensations. Inquiries indicated that subjects in the high-fear condition were much more frightened than those in the low-fear condition, indicating that the two sets of instructions were successful in producing different degrees of fear.

Following this arousal of fear, each subject was told that there would be a delay while the experimenter set up the equipment. The subject was told that he might wait in a room with others who were also participating in the experiment or he might wait alone and read a magazine or just rest. Subjects were asked to choose whether they would prefer waiting with others, alone, or whether they had no preference. They were also asked to rate the strength of their choices. This written measure of choice of waiting together (affiliation) or alone (nonaffiliation) was the dependent measure. As predicted, subjects who were more fearful were significantly more likely to want to affiliate with others than were subjects who were less fearful.

More important, for our purposes, was Schachter's finding that birth order of subjects was related to affiliative tendency. Specifically, it was discovered that firstborn subjects showed a significantly stronger tendency to affiliate (i.e., chose to wait together with others) than later-born subjects. Regardless of the size of the family in which they had been reared, firstborns showed greater affiliation than secondborns, secondborns showed greater affiliation than thirdborns, and so on.

These results were interpreted as a reflection of differences in the ways in which parents typically interact with firstborn as compared with later-born children. It is usually the case that parents are particularly solicitous and perhaps somewhat anxious about their first child. Since the first baby is the only child for some period of time, he is likely to receive plenty of attention. Parents are likely to come running and to pick the baby up whenever he shows signs of fear or distress. This concern on the part of parents tends to have a soothing effect, and the child comes to expect that the presence of other people is likely to reduce his fear. While there are no doubt exceptions, most parents are probably less anxious and less overprotective in their interactions with later-born children. For example, when their secondborn child starts to cry, they may not feel compelled to run to his aid immediately, as they did with their firstborn. Thus, a reasonable explanation of Schachter's findings may be that, for later-born children, the association between the presence of others and fear-reduction tends not to become so strong as it does for firstborns. If this is so, one would expect that firstborns will continue, as they grow up, to seek affiliative ways of reducing fear and anxiety and will rely on these behaviors to a greater extent than will later-borns. This kind of reasoning is very much in line with Adler's belief that a person's position in the family is likely to influence how other family members act toward him and this, in turn, affects the kinds of behavior patterns he is likely to develop.

MAJOR CONTRIBUTIONS

Adler made several contributions which are well worth noting. Doing away with the concept of psychic energy and instinctual determinants, he introduced a crude learning approach and went considerably further than Freud in stressing the importance of social and environmental factors. Perhaps his major contribution has been in the area of child development. His emphasis upon the effects of ordinal position, sibling rivalry, parental favoritism and displacement, the intricacies of family dynamics, and the importance of peers in personality development have all been widely accepted and have been useful for parents, teachers, psychotherapists, and other professionals who deal with children. He recognized the importance of treating significant adults when dealing with the problems of children and stressed the need for parents and teachers to try to make sure that each child, in the family or in the school situation, enjoyed his own particular claim to fame. Family therapy, now very popular as a strategy for dealing with children's behavior problems, was used by Adler long ago.

Many years before the women's liberation movement became popular, he introduced the concept of masculine protest to describe the effect upon women of holding a position which was regarded as inferior in Western culture.

Although some recent personality theorists, such as Harry Stack Sullivan and Karen Horney, have been labeled "neo-Freudian," they might also be considered "neo-Adlerian." Although they have adopted many of Freud's ideas, they have followed Adler in minimizing the importance of instincts and paying more attention to social and situational influences on personality.

SUMMARY AND ANALYSIS OF ADLER'S THEORY

The origins of two of Adler's three most central assumptions are explicit. The feelings of inadequacy or inferiority, presumably experienced by all human beings, result from the infant's long period of helplessness and dependence upon others. The striving for superiority or power is assumed to be a type of compensation; and Adler believed that the tendency to compensate for deficiencies was a biological characteristic of all living organisms. The assumption of social interest as a human potential and motivating force is not dealt with clearly in Adler's theory. While sometimes Adler spoke of the goal of social interest as an inborn human characteristic, at other times the concept was treated as a built-in characteristic of human society.

Adler's theory is much less systematic than that of Freud. The terms he introduces are defined less precisely, and their relationships to other concepts are not very carefully indicated. As a result, the constructs are quite general in nature, and there are many overlapping terms (e.g., "neurotic style of life," "mistaken style of life," "pampered style of life").

Another weakness of "Individual Psychology" as a system lies in the lack of specific lower-level constructs. For example, the individual's style of life is a very important and often-used construct in Adler's theory. But he provides no real classification system for characteristics of different styles of life. As a consequence, prediction and description of individual differences is quite limited. It seems, too, that different kinds of parental behavior—overindulgence, overprotection, overcontrol—all of which might be considered pampering behaviors, probably lead to somewhat different characteristics in the child. But these behaviors are not clearly specified as separate lower-level constructs. Only when Adler talks about the characteristic opportunities and problems associated with different ordinal positions in the family does he provide the kind of specific description that allows for the prediction of individual differences. Thus, tests of Adler's notions concerning the effects of birth order have led to fruitful and interesting research on the part of experimental social and personality psychologists.

Because many of Adler's constructs are somewhat broad and general in nature, they are difficult to operationalize. This is especially true for terms like "social interest." Does concern for one's society or for other people refer to social attitudes, to observable behaviors, to good intentions toward others, or to all three of these? How does one judge whether or not a given type of behavior reflects social interest? A person whose stated goal is to improve society and to better the quality of life for everyone might employ bombs and other terrorist tactics for this purpose; his destructive behavior may be motivated by good intentions and worthwhile goals. Another person might donate generously to good causes, but do so primarily in order to gain status and enhance his own image; here, the behavior is admirable but the motivation underlying the behavior is selfish. Clearly then, the concept of social interest is open to a number of conflicting interpretations and is very dependent upon the values held by the observer. Other Adlerian concepts, especially those which deal with childrearing practices, such as pampering, overprotection, and so on, can more easily be operationalized and measured (Rotter, 1962).

As mentioned above, Adler's theory tends to be lacking in specific constructs. As a consequence, Adler does not provide us with sufficient tools for describing individual differences in a systematic way. Like Freudian psychoanalysis, the vocabulary of Adler's content theory seems to be more useful for describing patterns of maladjusted behavior than for dealing with so-called normal personality characteristics or behavior patterns.

As a process theory, "Individual Psychology" is not very explicit about the ways in which behaviors are acquired or maintained. Adler implies, however, that behaviors tend to be learned from experience and through interaction with the environment. Although he does not concern himself with specifics of the learning process, he does indicate that the individual's experience determines his feelings of inadequacy (in what areas of life he feels most inadequate), his striving for superiority (what particular form this striving for power takes), the development of a style of life, the extent to which he relies upon distancing mechanisms to avoid failure, and so on.

Adler rejected the importance of instincts as proposed by Freud and stressed individual experiences and social influences. Adler was one of the first personality theorists to be regarded as an "environmentalist." Despite this important break with classical psychoanalytic theory, Adler shared Freud's belief that personality was pretty much fixed in early childhood and unlikely to change on the basis of experience once the basic character structure was set. While Freud's conviction that personality was formed during the first six years of life was based upon his instinct theory, Adler arrived at a similar conclusion on the basis of quite a different line of reasoning. Adler was one of the first to emphasize the ways in which personality affected perception and new learning. He thought that both the memory of past events and the perception of present circumstances were filtered or "screened" through the individual's style of life. Once the person's style of life was fixed — and this was thought to occur during the first years of childhood — he tended to accept experiences which were compatible with his style of life and reject experiences which were incompatible. For example, if his early experiences had led him to develop the notion that the world was essentially a competitive jungle in which one had to fight to make his way, this attitude would lead him to focus upon other people's competitive or hostile behaviors and to ignore or simply not notice acts of cooperation or kindness.

Adler believed that, even in adulthood, changes could occur if the individual recognized his mistaken view of the world and if he were encouraged to develop his social interest. In other words, change during adulthood could take place through understanding or insight. In his writings about the treatment of children, Adler tended to emphasize environmental treatment — that is, the treatment of parents, teachers, and others who deal with the child daily. A changed environment and new experiences were seen as the most efficient means of correcting a child's mistaken or maladjusted style of life.

Adler was not so concerned with broad environmental influences, such as poverty, as he was with specific and immediate environmental factors. Whether or not a condition such as poverty constituted a major handicap leading to an increased burden of inferiority feelings depended primarily upon the person's attitude toward his impoverished circumstances. For Adler, family members and others in the immediate environment were most important in determining this attitude. The same reasoning holds for physical handicaps; a crippled child or one who is mentally deficient may, given a healthy family atmosphere, develop a realistic style of life and appropriate ways of coping with his problem.

Attempts to compensate for or minimize inferiority feelings by striving for superiority and power constitute the major motivational variables in Adler's theory. Personality change is viewed as easier to accomplish with children than with adults. In this respect, Adler's treatment of children is similar to the procedures used by contemporary behavior therapists who maintain that behavior can be changed directly and efficiently without the development of insight.

In summary, Adler rejected Freud's notions concerning inherited instincts, their accompanying energy systems, and the centrality of sexual motivation. Instead he saw the feelings of inferiority, inadequacy, or insecurity of the infant and his striving to overcome that inferiority as the major source of human motivation. Opposed to this struggle for power or superiority was the person's social interest, or feeling for others.

In trying to overcome his feeling of inadequacy, each person develops a style of life based largely on family dynamics. This style of life becomes stabilized in childhood, acting as a perceptual screen for later experiences.

As a theory Adler's approach was very general, lacking sufficient terms to describe individual differences fully and lacking detailed statements of the processes by which personality characteristics are acquired and changed. Nevertheless, his many broad insights into human nature and many specific descriptions of childhood influences have had significant effects on other personality theorists, psychotherapists, and educational and child-training specialists.

6

Rogers' Self-Theory

Carl Rogers is a contemporary personality theorist whose approach differs in several respects from those we have discussed thus far. Because of his exclusive emphasis upon subjective experience and internal (rather than situational) processes, his is generally described as a "phenomenological" theory or a self-concept theory. In his writings, Rogers has been primarily concerned with explaining the changes that take place in the psychotherapy situation. Since his ideas about psychotherapy clearly show the influence of Otto Rank, still another early psychoanalytic theorist who broke away from the Freudian circle, it might be worthwhile to digress for a brief description of some of Rank's views.

Like others who grew uneasy about some of Freud's basic assumptions, Rank (1936) objected to the primacy of the sexual drive as a basic explanation of motivated behavior. Like Adler and others, he felt that unconscious processes were overemphasized and tended to reject the instinctual basis of Freudian theory. Adler's approach involved dealing with the patient's problem in a more direct, straightforward, and realistic fashion. This kind of psychotherapy, focusing more upon present and future events rather than on past experiences, tended to be considerably shorter in duration. Rank's differences with Freud were in some ways similar to Adler's and in some ways quite different.

Rank believed that detailed investigation of the individual's past history served no useful purpose; rather, it fixated the patient's attention on painful situations of the past, leaving him powerless to deal constructively with his current problems. He felt, therefore, that insight into the origin of current conflicts was neither necessary nor particularly useful in accomplishing change in a client. Rank noted that the typical strong "transference" reaction developed and encouraged in classical psychoanalytic therapy fostered highly dependent patient-therapist relationships and made therapy termination very difficult for patients. He asserted that, from the very beginning, the patient needed to be encouraged to change his behavior in the direction of independence. This principle of psychotherapy fitted in well with Rank's belief that the conflict between dependence and independence was a basic human problem. Fear of independence, a lack of confidence in one's ability to stand on one's own two feet, was seen as the source of one's problems in adjustment.

Instead of talking about catharsis and insight as necessary conditions for improvement in psychotherapy, Rank used the concept of willpower (constructive will) as an explanatory construct. Willpower was conceived as a basic human characteristic which allowed an individual to work toward obtaining his goals. Rank assumed that every person has the potential for developing constructive will but that it does not flower under adverse conditions. In order for willpower to develop, some "counter will" must be provided by the environment; people fail to develop willpower (similar to Adler's concept of pampering) when they grow up under conditions of no opposition or when the opposition to their asserting themselves is so great that the child's will is essentially crushed (similar to Adler's concept of rejection). The purpose of therapy is to awaken the patient's constructive will. The therapist, acting as counter will, discourages dependency in the patient and encourages or reinforces independence. This, then, is a kind of "relationship therapy" which focuses on the relationship between patient and therapist. Since Rank viewed the psychotherapy relationship as representative of the patient's relationships with other people, understanding and "working through" that relationship was treated as the central task of therapy. In order to keep the patient from becoming overly dependent upon the therapist, Rank engaged in relatively short-term psychotherapy and specified in advance the number of therapy sessions the patient could expect.

Rogers accepted Rank's general principle that therapy could proceed without an analysis of past experiences. Like Rank, Rogers emphasized the client's ability to solve his problems himself, with the therapist acting primarily as a catalyst, providing an atmosphere which encourages the development of independence and discourages the development of dependency upon the therapist.

BASIC ASSUMPTIONS

The first of Rogers' (1959) three basic assumptions is that the datum of psychology, the kind of material which the personality theorist must use in building his theory, is the individual's subjective experience. Like Adler, Rogers believes that what is crucial in terms of understanding a person's behavior is neither the circumstances surrounding the person's life nor the events in which he participates; what is most important is how the person perceives these circumstances and events. Rogers, however, takes a more extreme phenomenological position than Adler. He states that no one can truly or completely understand the internal frame of reference of another person, although that kind of data is the only meaningful kind of psychological data.

The second major assumption is that every person has an inborn tendency toward "self-actualization." Rogers defines this *actualizing tendency* as the inherent tendency of the individual to develop all his capacities in ways which seem to maintain or enhance the organism.

The third major assumption is that each person engages in an *organismic valuing process*. Experience is valued as positive or negative in reference to the actualizing tendency. The individual tends to approach positively valued experiences and to avoid negatively valued experiences. Further elaboration of these two constructs is necessary in order to understand the role they play in Rogers' theory of personality development.

PERSONALITY DEVELOPMENT

Self-Actualization and the Organismic Valuing Process

Self-actualization, as defined by Rogers, includes not only the satisfaction of biological needs and the learning of skills necessary for physical and social survival, but also development toward autonomy, independence, and a growing sense of self-determination. Self-actualization is Rogers' motivational construct, the single goal toward which all persons strive.

Rogers' definition of self-actualization is somewhat general in nature. How, then, does one know whether or not a particular behavior is actualizing for an individual? In answering this question, Rogers suggests that the person himself determines whether or not a given behavior is good for him on the basis of the feelings he experiences when contemplating or actually engaging in that behavior. If the person perceives an experience as one which maintains or enhances life, that experience is valued positively. If he perceives an experience as negating such maintenance or enhancement, it is valued negatively. Thus, each person is said to engage in an *organismic valuing process*. As mentioned above, Rogers suggests that individuals will continue to engage in positively valued behaviors and will avoid those behaviors which are valued negatively. It is assumed that, given little or no interference by other people or environmental pressures, each person is naturally capable of making correct decisions concerning what is best for him. In the section which follows we shall go on to discuss the ways in which external influences usually interfere with this organismic valuing process.

The Concept of Self

Rogers suggests that one of the most important processes in the development of personality is the development of the *self*. Early in life, the child begins to think about his own attributes and behaviors. His self-concept is made up of his habitual ways of thinking about himself. In accordance with the self-actualizing tendency, each person presumably engages in behaviors which are consistent with and which express his beliefs about himself, and rejects behaviors which are not compatible with his self-concept.

One important function served by the self, as described by Rogers, is a selective or screening function. (In this respect, Rogers' self is similar to Adler's style of life.) Only those new perceptions or ideas which are consistent with the existing self-concept can become part of the self. The person whose habits of thinking about himself are broad and inclusive will find that all kinds of emotional reactions, motivations, and behaviors are consistent with his self-concept. As a result of his broad self-image, he has no need or desire to ignore or avoid his own feelings of anger, lust, fear, love, and so on, nor is he inclined to avoid situations which arouse such feelings. His experiences and perceptions are, therefore, likely to be rich in variety. The person whose self-concept is narrow is, as a result, much less open to his experiences. If, for example, he thinks of himself as completely rational and not given to emotional outbursts, he will not be able to accept in himself even occasional feelings of rage, jealousy, sentimentality, and so on. Such strong spontaneous feelings and the behaviors which are likely to accompany them represent a threat and must be avoided in order to safeguard the existing self-concept. Likewise, the person who considers himself to be "pure" and above those who give in to their sexual appetites is likely to avoid sexual stimuli and ignore or distort his own lustful feelings.

The self-concept thus exerts an enormous influence upon both perceptions and actions. Rogers assumes that every individual has an innate capacity to be aware of *all* events in his environment, internal (one's own feelings and motivations) as well as external. A person's perception (actual awareness) of his own behaviors and the events influencing him must be accurate and reasonably complete if he is to be able to direct and control his life in a satisfying way. Rogers introduces the term *subception* to explain how people react to certain kinds of events without being fully aware of them. Thus, a person who is uncomfortable about his own sexuality may *subceive* sexual cues in a social situation and avoid or distort such signals, without really being aware of what he's doing. The subception concept is Rogers' way of dealing with the notion of "unconscious" awareness. Subception of threat allows the person to protect his self-concept. At the same time, according to Rogers, it keeps the individual from thinking about and realistically dealing with any problems he may have. Nevertheless, Rogers' theory is quite optimistic with regard to the possibility of personality change. He suggests that self-concepts often change as a result of new experiences and feedback from other people. Rogerian psychotherapy is designed to create conditions which encourage increased awareness and the development of greater self-acceptance (a broader self-concept) on the part of the client.

Need for Positive Regard

One of Rogers' major constructs is the *need for positive regard*. Rogers suggests that every individual has a need for other people to regard him positively. While he does not deal specifically with the question of whether this need is an inborn or learned characteristic of human beings, he does suggest that it is universal. According to the theory, this need can, in some individuals, become *too* important and can conflict with the need for self-actualization. The child, from the very beginning, experiences satisfaction and happiness whenever he receives positive feedback, such as warmth, liking, acceptance, respect, and so on, from significant persons in his environment. Negative feedback, such as hostility, rejection, coldness, and lack of respect, makes the child unhappy. Gradually, his need for positive regard grows stronger and he learns to seek positive feedback in a more active fashion.

Need for Self-Regard

The *need for self-regard* follows developmentally from the need for positive regard. This need for self-regard develops as the child learns to judge his own behaviors as good or bad on the basis of others' evaluations. In other words, the child comes to evaluate positively those of his behaviors which lead to positive feedback from others who are important to him and to evaluate negatively behaviors which lead to negative feedback from others. Thus, each person has two bases for evaluating his own behavior: innate evaluations (the organismic valuing process) and learned evaluations (the standards of significant others are "introjected" and become the criteria for self-evaluation). Rogers suggests that in the healthy person these innate and learned evaluations operate together — that is, behaviors which are satisfying and "feel right" to the individual are also likely to be acceptable and positively evaluated by others.

Conditions of Worth

Rogers states that, in connection with the developing needs for positive regard and self-regard, each person develops a set of *conditions of worth*. These conditions of worth are standards of conduct which the person must meet in order to experience self-acceptance. Individuals vary in terms of the number of conditions of worth they develop. Some people are able to feel comfortable and worthy so long as they live up to a few important standards of conduct. Others develop a great number of "rules" or conditions of acceptance and experience distress whenever they cannot act in accordance with these multiple standards. Whether one develops few or many conditions of worth depends ultimately upon interpersonal experiences in one's immediate environment. Rogers suggests that the ideal environment is one in which the person experiences unconditional positive regard. If others always react positively and indicate their respect and liking for the individual despite his weaknesses and occasional human failings, he is likely to develop a relatively broad self-concept with no necessary conditions of worth. Most people, according to Rogers, do not grow up in this positive and accepting atmosphere. Rather, they learn that others like and respect them only if they behave in certain ways. As we shall see below, Rogers believes that it is the task of the psychotherapist to create a situation in which the client experiences unconditional positive regard; presumably, this allows the client to find some solutions for his problems by bringing to light the standards which the client has introjected.

MALADJUSTMENT

Rogers considers all forms of maladjustment to be a consequence of faulty experience which interferes with the natural development of the healthy, self-actualizing personality. Rogers suggests a conflict model of disorder. Maladjusted behavior, according to the theory, occurs as a result of conflict between a person's evaluative thoughts based on his own emotional and physiological responses and the evaluative thoughts of others which he has adopted. Rogers believes that it is the learned evaluative thoughts which lie at the core of the disorder. These learned evaluations control and limit one's perceptions and behaviors.

Although his vocabulary is quite different from Freud's, Rogers' notions about conflict, anxiety, and defensive behaviors are quite similar to Freud's model of maladjustment. While they describe the origin of psychological conflict in different ways, Rogers shares Freud's belief that (1) conflict leads to anxiety, and (2) the anxious individual then learns behaviors which serve to reduce or terminate anxiety.

Rogers suggests that when a person has learned to think of a particular kind of response as bad or unacceptable when it actually seems to be inherently satisfying, or vice versa (when his learned values indicate that a behavior is good when it seems to him to be undesirable), he will experience anxiety whenever he is in situations which arouse this conflict. In Rogers' language, the person is *vulnerable* in those situations and subceives them as threatening. In order to avoid anxiety, the individual may employ one of two types of psychological defenses: *denial to awareness* or *distortion in awareness*. Using denial to awareness, the person ignores what is really happening in anxiety-arousing situations. Distortion in awareness involves the person's thinking inaccurately about threatening situations and misinterpreting events in ways which are more acceptable to him. Rogers feels that these defensive habits lead to further difficulties because they prevent the person from thinking constructively about his problems. Moreover, if the incongruence between the individual's *ideal self* (what he would like to become according to his own self-actualizing tendency) and his *experienced self* (the kind of person he should be according to the evaluative thoughts he has adopted from others) becomes too great, disorganized behavior may occur. In the disorganized state, the person engages in contradictory behavior, sometimes acting in accordance with his own valuing process and sometimes behaving in accordance with others' wishes or expectations. This inconsistency in behavior is anxiety-arousing in itself and is likely to lead to interpersonal problems.

ROGERIAN PSYCHOTHERAPY

Rogers refers to his method of psychotherapy as client-centered and nondirective. By using the term "client-centered," he stresses the phenomenological nature of his approach, the necessity of trying to see the world through the eyes of the client. While it is questionable whether any kind of psychotherapeutic intervention can be truly nondirective, the stated goal of Rogerian therapy is to provide an atmosphere in which the client can essentially solve his problems for himself. Rogers feels that interpreting to the patient the meaning of his behavior tends to force the patient to see himself from the therapist's point of view, rather than from his own.

NON DIRECTIONAL

In discussing the ideal conditions for therapy, Rogers states a number of attitudinal and behavioral prescriptions for the psychotherapist. For example, the therapist should, himself, be relatively free of conflict. If the therapist is vulnerable to feelings of anxiety in the therapy situation, his vulnerability and defensiveness are likely to reduce his effectiveness. The therapist is also expected to experience unconditional positive regard for the client. Like Freud, Rogers believes that it is important for the therapist to be accepting and nonevaluative in relation to the client. If the therapist is successful in this regard, the client will come to trust him and will feel free to talk about even the most private and sensitive matters. The therapist must be consistently friendly, warm, and attentive so that the client knows that he is liked and respected despite any faults or unworthy motives he might reveal in the therapy situation.

It is the therapist's task to experience empathic understanding of the client's internal frame of reference and to convey this understanding to the client. Rather than using direct interpretive techniques, the therapist listens to what the client has to say and reflects back to him the client's own feelings. The purpose of this technique is to allow the client to gain insight into his own thoughts and feelings and to encourage him to explore them further.

As mentioned earlier, Rogers rejects the importance of exploring the client's past experiences, feeling that this serves no useful purpose for either the patient or the therapist. In fact, Rogers believes that such a diagnostic orientation on the part of the therapist is likely to interfere with his understanding of the client's present feelings.

As he progresses in therapy, the client is expected to express his feelings more and more and to gain a better understanding of them. The natural outcome of this understanding, according to Rogers, is the integration of the self and the elimination of conflicting emotions. Since no conditions of worth are set up in the therapy situation, the client feels comfortable and is able to admit all his experiences and feelings into awareness. He can, therefore, begin to examine and think accurately about his experiences and solve those internal conflicts which have been interfering with his self-actualization.

Rogers' therapy methods have been criticized by others and have been found vulnerable on several counts. Some psychologists have suggested that any kind of psychotherapy is to some degree directive and that values of the psychotherapist can never be entirely eliminated from the therapy situation. Even the most nondirective Rogerian therapist responds selectively to what the client says and reflects back to him only part of that material. The importance of nonverbal cues in psychotherapy is quite well documented experimentally, and this kind of evidence suggests that, without being aware that he is doing so, the therapist may be frequently shaping the client's behaviors by means of such cues. In addition, Rogers has been criticized (along with other "insight" therapists) for his assumption that changes in a client's behavior in the therapy situation generalize to other situations.

Rogerian therapy tends to be of relatively short duration. It is apparent that what is required of the therapist is more an attitude or a particular frame of mind than a special form of long-term training. As a result, these techniques are widely used by social workers, school guidance personnel, and clergy involved in counseling activities.

Rogers has contributed a great deal to the exploration of the process of psychotherapy through his emphasis upon the importance of psychotherapy research. Using recordings of actual therapy sessions, he collected material which could be carefully studied for research purposes and which has proved useful in the training of psychotherapists.

REPRESENTATIVE RESEARCH

A study by Chodorkoff (1954) provides some good examples of the kind of techniques which have been used to operationalize Rogerian constructs. Chodorkoff tested several of Rogers' hypotheses regarding the relationships among three variables: adjustment, accuracy of self-perception, and defensiveness. He hypothesized that the greater the agreement between an individual's self-description and an objective description of him, the better would be the personal adjustment of that individual and the less perceptual defensiveness he would show. Defensiveness is defined here as a perceptual phenomenon, a process which prevents the person from becoming aware of threatening events.

The Q-sort technique, a method used frequently by Rogers and his colleagues, provided a measure of the accuracy of subjects' self-descriptions. The subjects were thirty college students. Each subject was given 125 descriptive statements and asked to sort them along a continuum according to the degree to which they described him. These same 125 statements were sorted by judges, whose ratings of the subjects were based on biographical material and psychological test data. The projective tests used included the Rorschach, the Thematic Apperception Test, and a word association test (see Chapter 9). The judges' descriptions of the subject were correlated with the subject's self-description to obtain an accuracy of self-description score.

Chodorkoff selected from each subject's word association test ten words which were considered to be neutral and ten which were considered to be threatening or anxiety-provoking words for that person. In order to measure perceptual defensiveness, these words were presented to the subject by tachistoscope, a projection device which exposes material on a screen very rapidly for very short intervals. Recognition thresholds (in this case, the length of time the word was on the screen before it could be recognized) were calculated for neutral and threatening words. The assumption underlying this kind of measure is that failure to recognize particular words or taking a very long time to recognize them indicates defensiveness. The difference between the recognition thresholds for the neutral and threatening words gave a mean perceptual defensiveness score. (Subjects who showed much greater difficulty in recognizing threatening as compared with neutral words were considered to be high in perceptual defensiveness.)

Adjustment ratings were made by the judges on the basis of the projective test data. The results supported all of the hypotheses. Accuracy of self-description was significantly related to perceptual defensiveness scores and adjustment, and perceptual defensiveness scores also related to adjustment. That is, subjects who were more accurate in their self-descriptions tended to be better adjusted and showed less perceptual defensiveness than subjects whose self-descriptions were less accurate.

Chodorkoff himself suggested that the major problem with this study lies in the contamination of the judges who made the adjustment ratings from the same test data that they used for their Q-sort descriptions of the subjects. That is, judges already had knowledge of the Q-sort descriptions when they made the adjustment ratings. Their judgments concerning adjustment could have been influenced in favor of their hypotheses because of this prior knowledge. The perceptual defensiveness scores were not contaminated in this way, since they were obtained independently. However, even this measure is somewhat problematical, since the judges made use of the word association tests from which the neutral and threatening words were selected. It is very difficult to determine to what extent such contamination and overlap among the measures used actually affected the results. Taken at face value, however, these results show support for Rogers' hypotheses.

MAJOR CONTRIBUTIONS

Rogers' most important contribution lies in the development of methodology for psychotherapy research and his emphasis on the importance of such research. His work in the areas of psychotherapy training and practice has been influential in increasing both the acceptability of short-term therapy and, as a result of his simplified training process, the potential number of therapy practitioners. Counseling psychologists in clerical and educational settings have profited from these training techniques. Some of the impetus for contemporary self-theories and research dealing with the self-concept can be traced to the work of Rogers and his colleagues. He has also been a recognized leader among a group of psychologists who regard themselves primarily as "humanists."

SUMMARY AND ANALYSIS OF ROGERS' THEORY

Rogers' assumptions concerning human nature, the universality of the self-actualizing tendency, and the overriding importance of subjective experience are quite explicit. Likewise, he provides definitions for his major constructs. In many instances, however, these definitions are highly abstract in nature and are not anchored in observables. This is especially true of his more general constructs. As a consequence, constructs such as the self-actualizing tendency — which is his major motivational construct—are subject to a variety of interpretations, making it difficult for workers in the field to arrive at a common agreement concerning the real meaning of such terms.

In general, Rogers has linked all of his constructs together and has specified the direction of the relationships between the various constructs. For example, internal conflict leads to vulnerability and defensive behaviors; the absence of positive regard from others leads to the setting up of conditions of worth; the presence of many conditions of worth interferes with the self-actualizing tendency.

A basic difficulty with Rogers' theoretical orientation is that most of his constructs are defined in terms of some internal process (experiencing of positive regard, the organismic valuing process, etc.) and are difficult to measure. Since psychotherapy research has been of prime interest to Rogers, he and his students have devised operations for measuring those concepts which are most closely related to the conduct of psychotherapy and the criteria for psychotherapeutic success. For example, unconditional positive regard is measured by having several therapists rate the degree to which a particular therapist tends to directively control his client's behavior in therapy. The less directive the therapist's behavior appears to the raters, the greater the unconditional positive regard is said to exist in the therapy situation. Good agreement among raters in this kind of study indicates that such measurements can be made reliably.

Rogers' theory is primarily a process theory. His interest in content categories is limited to a few broad variables. The major differences among individuals, according to Rogers, involve the amount of discrepancy between ideal and experienced self, the amount of anxiety and subsequent defense, and the amount of self-actualizing experience. (These content variables are considered important in terms of Rogerian psychotherapy, which is aimed at decreasing the discrepancy between ideal and experienced self, reducing the amount of anxiety and defensiveness, and increasing the amount of self-actualizing experience.) Except for these very broad categories, then, Rogers provides us with relatively few terms which would be useful in describing the great variety of individual differences in human behavior.

The Rogerian process theory, designed primarily to describe and explain very general processes involved in psychotherapy, indicates the importance of subjective experience. Rogers emphasizes the ways in which the individual's experiences may enhance or interfere with natural growth potentials. Nevertheless, he does not discuss how specific

behaviors, traits, or needs are acquired or developed, and he does assume some important motives to be innate potentials.

Rogers' explanatory constructs appear to be more exclusively internal
than those of any other theorist described in this book. His emphasis
upon internal determinants, however, is not consistent. In discussing
psychotherapy, Rogers generally emphasizes situational variables, particularly those related to the behavior of the therapist. His research implies, for example, that differences in clients' behavior during therapy
occur as a function of the degree of unconditional positive regard con-
veyed by the therapist. However, when he is talking about behavior,
experience, or feelings outside of therapy, Rogers relies almost exclusively on internal processes. Although he sometimes implies that certain
situations are more likely than others to produce threat or promote
growth, he generates no predictions from specific kinds of situations.

In summary, Rogers has developed a process theory with a strong focus on the broad general processes involved in psychotherapy and adjustment. It allows for the description of individual differences only in
very general terms and only for a few variables. This, however, is what
he set out to do. He has done it by assuming for everyone a strong, inborn, positive motivation which will make for creative behavior and
freedom from serious internal conflict, but which is inhibited by non-
constructive experiences. Psychotherapy is a process which releases this
inhibited force and allows the person to self-actualize. Whether or not
his assumptions are valid or his process theory for enhancing positive
growth is correct or useful will only be determined when ways are developed to measure his constructs more satisfactorily.

7

Maslow's Holistic Theory

Abraham Maslow (1962; 1970) is one of a number of contemporary psychologists, including Rogers, whose views concerning personality and human nature are most often referred to as "humanistic." The humanistic approach, which currently is enjoying considerable popularity, grew out of a strong discontent with the fact that earlier theories, particularly Freudian psychoanalysis, tended to be more concerned with sickness or maladjustment than with human capacities for psychological health and happiness. In addition to his dissatisfaction with theories based almost exclusively upon the study of neurotic individuals, Maslow was skeptical of the attempts being made by experimental psychologists to explain human motivation on the basis of laboratory studies of lower animals. It seemed to Maslow that both psychoanalytic theory and laboratory psychology dealt only with one class of human motivation: the attempt to avoid or escape from pain and discomfort. What was lacking was a theory of motivation which focused not only on the negative and self-protective motives, but also on the positive, "higher" motives which characterize human beings. Maslow's theory, then, represents an attempt to build upon the theories dealing with so-called "deficiency needs" by including, in a hierarchical theory of motivation, consideration of "growth needs," which are seen as equally important in gaining an understanding of human behavior.

BASIC ASSUMPTIONS

Like Adler, who influenced him, Maslow's theory is holistic in nature; that is, he views the individual as an integrated, organized whole. For this reason, he believes that it is not useful to study human motivations or drives in an isolated, one-at-a-time fashion. Maslow states very forcefully that the assumption that *all* drives are essentially like physiological drives, such as the hunger drive, is wrong. No matter how much we know about hunger as a basic motivating force, it will not lead to a full understanding of the need for love.

Maslow assumes that almost all of our acts and conscious wishes represent multiple motivations rather than serving one need at a time. For this reason, it is necessary to study relationships among motivations rather than focusing on isolated drives or desires. He describes the human being as "a wanting animal" and believes that rarely does an individual reach a state of complete satisfaction except for a very short time. Once a desire is satisfied, according to Maslow's view, another desire emerges to take its place. Human wants or needs seem to be arranged in a kind of hierarchy in which some motivations must be satisfied before other motivations appear.

Finally, Maslow believes that psychologists should not base their motivational theories only on the study of unhealthy, neurotic people. Health is not just the opposite of disease or the absence of maladjustment; it is a condition worthy of study in its own right. Motivational theories, therefore, must deal with the highest capacities of healthy individuals as well as the distorted or thwarted desires of the unhealthy.

BASIC NEEDS

Maslow has suggested a hierarchical theory of human motivation. This hierarchy consists of a series of basic needs, some of which are more "prepotent" than others — that is, more basic in the sense that these needs must be satisfied before other needs can emerge as important motivators of behavior.

Physiological Needs

The physiological needs are the most prepotent of all needs. Despite the fact that experimental psychologists have focused on physiological needs in their laboratory studies, Maslow believes that these needs should be considered unusual rather than typical of other motivational states. Unlike other (higher) needs, these needs are relatively independent of each other, and they can be localized in the body; therefore, they can be studied in a more isolated fashion than other needs.

If an individual's physiological needs are unsatisfied, he will, of course, be dominated by them, and all other needs are trivial. The person who is extremely hungry has no other interest but food. To paraphrase Maslow, man lives by bread alone only when there is no bread. An individual may be lacking many things—food, safety, love, and esteem—but because of the prepotency of physiological needs, the person will in most cases hunger for food more strongly then for anything else.

When the physiological needs are gratified on a regular basis, they no longer serve as active determinants or organizers of behavior. They are still potentially important motivators which may become dominant whenever physiological satisfactions are cut off by circumstances, such as in an emergency situation. But once a need or want is satisfied, it is no longer a need. According to Maslow, the "organism is dominated and its behavior organized only by unsatisfied needs" (1970, p. 38). Thus, when the physiological needs are satisfied, a new set of needs, the safety needs, become dominant.

Safety Needs

The safety needs include the needs for stability, security, dependency, protection, freedom from fear and anxiety, and so on. The average person in our society prefers the world to be orderly and predictable, rather than chaotic. This is particularly obvious in the case of children who appear to need some optimal amount of structure, rules, and limitations in order to function effectively and without great anxiety and confusion. But among adults as well there exist numerous examples of concern for safety. Most people clearly prefer jobs which are steady and secure. We invest in various kinds of insurance and save money for a rainy day. And most people seem to feel comfortable and happy in familiar situations and experience anxiety when confronted with the unknown. The healthy adult in our society is, according to Maslow, able to satisfy his safety needs relatively easily, so that these needs are dominant only in the case of real emergencies. However, neurotic individuals and people who are oppressed by unfortunate social conditions, such as poverty and chronic unemployment, are very strongly motivated by safety needs on a regular basis. These needs are of central importance whenever an individual perceives the world (realistically or unrealistically) as hostile, threatening, or overwhelming. The person who would be clinically described as having an obsessive-compulsive neurosis provides a striking example of an individual dominated by his safety needs. Such a person tries to order and stabilize his world so that everything is stable, familiar, and perfectly predictable. Any event which is unexpected is perceived as dangerous and is likely to lead to a great deal of anxiety and perhaps panic reactions.

Maslow points out, too, that the threat of civil disorder in our society is likely, for most people, to cause a regression from higher needs to the more prepotent safety needs. Our recent history of civil disturbances among ghetto residents and the student demonstrations of the 1960s indeed led to a rising tide of fear and a public outcry for greater police power to restore law and order. Under such circumstances, Maslow suggests that many people may be willing to accept even such drastic measures as a dictatorship or a military takeover as effective means of restoring order to their world. Even healthy human beings will tend to respond to danger with regression to the level of safety needs. But Maslow thinks that this kind of regression is most characteristic of people who are "living near the safety line"—people for whom safety needs, rather than higher needs, are always relatively important. It is these people who are particularly disturbed by threats to authority and institutions.

Belongingness and Love Needs

At the next higher level are the needs for love and a sense of belonging, which emerge if both the physiological and the safety needs of the individual are fairly well gratified. According to Maslow, the thwarting of these needs is the basis for most if not all forms of maladjustment.

Maslow suggests that the recent popularity of T-groups and other personal growth groups and communes may be motivated by unsatisfied longings for love and intimacy and the need to overcome the feelings of loneliness and alienation which are widespread in our highly mobile, rapidly changing society. Likewise, he believes that many groups of young people involved in rebellious movements directed against "the establishment" are at least partially motivated by the desire for a sense of belonging, a need for banding together against a common enemy.

Esteem Needs

Esteem needs appear to become important once the need for love and a sense of belonging is at least partially satisfied. Thus, Maslow's esteem needs include two related sets of motivations: (1) the need to be strong, competent, and confident about one's own abilities and personal characteristics; and (2) the need for recognition, status, and the respect or esteem of other people.

When the esteem needs are satisfied, the individual feels self-confident and worthy. When they are thwarted or not sufficiently satisfied, he feels inferior, weak, and unworthy. Like Adler, Maslow believes that such negative feelings about oneself tend to lead to very unfortunate consequences. Some persons respond by becoming completely discouraged and passive. Others attempt to compensate or engage in neurotic behaviors in an attempt to protect their self-image.

The Need for Self-Actualization

The clear emergence of this highest of all human needs usually depends upon prior satisfaction of the physiological, safety, love, and esteem needs. Self-actualization is defined as the desire for self-fulfillment, the need to live up to one's potentials, whatever they may be. Maslow believes that even if all the other needs are satisfied, the person will become restless and will not really be content and happy unless he is doing whatever he is best suited for, whatever activity best expresses his true nature. The need for self-actualization may be expressed in countless forms. For some people, self-actualization consists of artistic endeavors; for others, it involves becoming the best possible parent, developing athletic skills, inventing things, developing a satisfying philosophy of life, engaging in attempts to improve social conditions or political institutions, and so on. A more complete description of the characteristics Maslow believes to be typical of self-actualizing individuals appears below. But first, let us go on for a moment to discuss some characteristics of the basic needs and their hierarchical arrangement.

Additional Characteristics of the Basic Needs

Maslow is careful to point out that his suggested need hierarchy is not rigid, although it appears to fit the ordering of needs that is characteristic of most people in our society. He provides a number of illustrations of exceptions to the typical order. For example, he suggests that there are some people whose need for self-esteem seems to be more important (more prepotent) than their need for love. This is the most common reversal he has found in his studies and observations. But, for such people, self-esteem seems to be more a means than an end in itself; they try to be strong and competent in order to be loved by others.

There are also people whose level of aspiration seems to have been permanently lowered as a result of repeated bad experiences. For such individuals, the higher goals are unimportant and the person appears to be satisfied as long as just his physiological needs are met. No higher needs are ever active determinants of behavior.

Another important exception involves the importance, to some people, of higher social values or ideals. There are always people in any society who in some sense become martyrs, who give up everything and ignore many basic needs for the sake of strongly held beliefs or ideals. The hierarchy of needs, then, is designed to describe the typical rather than the universal ordering of human motivations.

Although Maslow's theory essentially involves the classification of needs into five categories, he is careful to point out that most behavior is motivated by more than a single need. For example, the act of making love may simultaneously express a desire for sexual satisfaction, a desire to convince oneself or others of one's masculinity or femininity, a desire to gain love and affection, a desire for dominance, and so on. Human motivation must, for Maslow, be studied in all its complexity in order for us to achieve a real understanding of human nature.

Finally, Maslow suggests that needs are not *necessarily* conscious or unconscious. In the average person, however, he believes that needs are more often unconscious than conscious. Maslow agrees with Freud's view of everyday conscious desires as "surface indicators of more basic needs." For example, a person's conscious desire for an ice cream cone may signify an underlying desire for love (of which the individual is unaware at the time), or it may be merely a wish for something that is cool and tastes good. It is the underlying and usually unconscious desires which are most important in Maslow's theory.

PSYCHOLOGICAL HEALTH AND MALADJUSTMENT

Maslow discusses the concept of "gratification health" (or "happiness health"). He is like Adler, Rogers, and others who have suggested that there is a positive growth tendency in people which might serve as an index of mental health. Specifically, Maslow believes that the degree of basic need gratification is positively correlated with the degree of psychological health. Thus, "other things being equal, a man who is safe and belongs and is loved will be healthier than a man who is safe, and belongs, but who is rejected and unloved. And if in addition, he wins respect and admiration, and because of this, develops his self-respect, then he is still *more* healthy, self-actualizing, or fully human" (1970, p. 68). Failure to satisfy needs or danger to our ways of satisfying them leads to defensive behavior. Some defensive behavior appears as pathological symptoms even though it is an attempt to cope with the danger. Other pathological symptoms are primarily expressive of feelings of helplessness and despair.

The neurotic person, according to Maslow, is one who lacks the basic need satisfactions that can come only from other people. Therefore, this kind of person is more dependent on others and less autonomous; he is more shaped by environmental forces than by his own intrinsic nature. For the healthy person, the environment is not such a strong determining factor; rather, it is primarily "a means to the person's self-actualizing ends" (1970, p. 68).

SELF-ACTUALIZING PEOPLE

Believing that psychologists have too long been preoccupied with studying sickness and maladjustment, Maslow and his colleagues have devoted themselves to the study of individuals whom they consider to be psychologically healthy. Essentially, Maslow presents rather global or holistic impressions of people (real people and some historical figures) who seemed to him to be healthy and self-actualizing. Often without utilizing traditional clinical techniques such as formal interviews or psychological tests, he attempts to describe his subjects in an informal fashion, in the same way that one might convey impressions about friends and acquaintances. Older subjects and, of course, historical figures were studied most informally; younger subjects were interviewed, questioned, and tested more systematically. The following are the major characteristics which Maslow reported as typical of self-actualizing persons.

The self-actualizing individual shows good perception of reality. He is able to judge people and situations correctly and efficiently, and is able to detect phoniness and dishonesty in others. There are several reasons underlying this ability. The healthy individual has greater tolerance for ambiguity and less fear of the unknown than does the unhealthy person. And because of this relative lack of fear, he is less likely to distort reality in a self-protective fashion.

Another characteristic of the self-actualizing person is his acceptance of self, of other people, and of the natural world. Because of their relative lack of guilt, shame, and anxiety, such people are able to accept their own shortcomings as well as human weakness or frailties in general.

Self-actualizing people are described as spontaneous and natural. They dislike pretense and artificiality and, although they are often willing to observe society's conventions, they do not feel totally bound by such conventions.

These individuals are also described as problem-centered rather than ego-centered. They tend to have some mission in life—some type of work to do which is absorbing and important to them. Related to this problem-centeredness is a concern wih ethical or philosophical questions and human values.

Self-actualizing people typically display a need for solitude and privacy. Their need for privacy indeed seems to be stronger than that of the average person. Related to this is their ability to remain calm, aloof, and dignified in difficult situations, and their capacity to be objective and logical when those behaviors are called for.

One of the qualities of the self-actualizing person which Maslow emphasizes is his autonomy. Having received plenty of love and respect in the past, the individual is free to act relatively independently of these needs in the present. Self-development and inner growth are more important than anything that the environment can provide, including prestige, honors, status, public acclaim, and love.

The self-actualized person has a freshness of appreciation of the good things in life, which allows him to continue to see the world with new eyes. His subjective experience is thus very rich, and the everyday business of living and working remains interesting and even exciting to him. In addition, this kind of individual often has what Maslow calls "peak experiences." A peak experience involves a tremendous intensification of "any experience in which there is loss of self or transcendence of it"—for example, an intense sensuous experience, self-forgetful enjoyment of art or music, intense concentration on intellectual problems, and so on. Peak experiences seemed to be fairly common for most, although not all, of Maslow's self-actualizing subjects.

Self-actualizers are described as having a genuine desire to help the human race, and they have a strong basic identification with and sympathy for all humanity. In terms of their interpersonal relations with other individuals, these people are described by Maslow as having deeper and more profound interpersonal relations than do other, non-self-actualizing adults. They tend to have especially strong ties with just a few individuals, and these friends also tend to be self-actualizers.

All of the people studied by Maslow displayed a great deal of creativeness or originality. This was expressed in a variety of ways, and it is described as an attitude toward one's endeavors, a spirit or quality of doing things.

In discussing the attributes of self-actualizing individuals, Maslow often seems to be describing a super-species, a group of men and women who stand above and apart from real mortals. In a sense, that is exactly his intention. Yet he freely admits that all his self-actualizing subjects display the usual number of human failings, such as vanity, temper outbursts, occasional ruthlessness, and stubborn pride. Completely absorbed in some work or activity, they are often unintentionally rude, inconsiderate, and selfish. For Maslow, there are no perfect human beings; but self-actualizing individuals are described as very good indeed.

PSYCHOTHERAPY

Maslow's writings on the subject of psychotherapy are focused more on the goals of good therapy than on particular therapeutic strategies or specific techniques. Emphasizing that his own experience involves mainly the briefer therapies, Maslow suggests that the gratification of basic needs is the most important aim of psychotherapy of this type. Such need gratification is expected to lead to the ultimate positive goal of therapy which is self-actualization.

According to Maslow, the basic needs of safety, belongingness, love, and respect can be satisfied only by other people. For this reason, the quality of the patient-therapist relationship is of great importance. Essentially, the unhealthy individual needs to be supplied in therapy with the satisfactions that he should have received in other good human relationships. Maslow defines the sick or maladjusted person as someone whose needs for love and respect have not been sufficiently gratified in the past.

Maslow believes that psychotherapy is like any other good relationship—like marriage, or a partnership, or a good friendship. Because of this similarity to other interpersonal relationships, therapy is one way of preparing the patient for future healthy relationships; it should serve as a model for interpersonal encounters outside of the therapy situation.

Finally, Maslow sees considerable promise in traditional group therapy and in the newer kinds of personal growth groups, such as T-groups and encounter groups. He feels that group therapies have several notable advantages. For example, the group experience may be quite effective in reducing a person's feelings of isolation. Simply learning that other people have similar problems may be very reassuring. In addition, groups provide an opportunity for one to learn how to establish good relationships with a number of people at once.

MAJOR CONTRIBUTIONS

Maslow's ideas about the nature of personality have been quite influential among contemporary humanistic psychologists. Humanistic psychology represents a turning away from traditional scientific methodology toward more subjective, value-oriented ways of observing and trying to understand human behavior. Maslow's ideas about basic needs, and especially his elaboration of the concept of self-actualization, are considered important contributions by many psychologists who feel that we should be concerned with the study of healthy as well as neurotic individuals. And because of his emphasis on the importance of understanding psychological health, Maslow's notions have had a significant impact upon people involved in group approaches (T-groups, encounter groups, human-potential training groups) whose goal is the release of basic human potentials for growth and self-actualization.

SUMMARY AND ANALYSIS OF MASLOW'S THEORY

Maslow's theory is fairly well systematized with explicit assumptions, reasonably well-defined constructs, and some relationships among constructs made explicit. However, the theory is very general and it is weak on antecedents and consequences. Consequently, prediction of behavior is difficult, if not impossible. Perhaps this is not surprising; Maslow is probably not too concerned with prediction but more with description and the expression of a set of values regarding what is psychological health.

While he states rather generally that the strength of a basic need depends, at least in part, on the gratification of earlier needs in the hierarchy, he is not all explicit about how much gratification, what kind, or when. An individual develops a need for self-actualization when his needs for love, recognition, and self-esteem are gratified. But how much gratification of love and recognition are necessary? It seems intuitively obvious that there are some people who not only get tremendous quantities of recognition and love but whose needs seem to be insatiable. The basic needs themselves are considered to be instinctual in nature. That is, they will arise naturally because of inborn characteristics of the individual when earlier needs are gratified. Of course this eliminates the necessity for stating specific antecedents, and it is in this area that Maslow's theory is particularly deficient as a system.

The basic constructs of Maslow's theory are needs. He defines his hierarchy of needs in a general, nontechnical fashion. They are easy to understand but would be more difficult to measure. For example, self-actualized people are creative, but what is creativity? It is easy to decide that a great composer is creative, but how is creativity measured in a schoolteacher, a factory worker, and a housewife? Not everyone can be a great composer. Because of the absence of specific, concrete definitions, some of his statements may appear contradictory. For example, Maslow says that the self-actualized person is warm, loving, and identified with other people, but he also says he is aloof and detached. Is this true, or is it merely Maslow's subjective opinion? Because of the difficulty in measuring Maslow's concepts, some of the basic aspects of his process theory cannot be tested. Do the basic needs really follow in order as the result of gratification of earlier ones? Do the different kinds of characteristics of the supposedly self-actualized person really vary together? That is, do they vary in such a way that when one is present the others are also present? Perhaps Maslow has only given us a picture of an idealized person whom he believes to be the kind of person we should all strive to be—his description of what psychological health "really" is. The only evidence he presents is the description of specific individuals based on rather subjective case studies, and these individuals perhaps represent only a few isolated people whom he has picked out because they fit his conception. The idea of self-actualization is attractive to many people but probably means as many different things to different people as does the word "good" or "successful."

Of course, as Maslow sees it, many people never advance to the stage where they have a strong motive for self-actualization. Some never even appear to develop a strong need for love or achievement. It is not enough to say that such individuals simply have not received enough gratification of earlier needs, if one wants to help them. Rather, one would have to know *specifically* what kinds of experiences they had missed out on. Perhaps they have been rewarded at earlier points in their life for behaviors which have become so dominant as to preclude the learning of alternatives which will lead to love, recognition, creativity, and so on. In order to make the theory more useful in application, it would have to be far more specific and detailed. Both the content theory and the process theory are quite general, and both are limited. The process theory is limited to need gratification and the content theory to a description of a hierarchy of basic needs, but Maslow leaves out many other important facets of personality or individual differences.

Maslow's treatment of the immediate situation is somewhat unique. He feels that the lower an individual stands in the hierarchy of basic needs, the more he responds to the immediate situation. The closer he gets to being self-actualized, the more his behaviors spring from internal sources and the less attention he pays to the immediate situation. It is questionable whether there is any evidence for this or whether, in fact, this is a logical and reasonable assumption.

For purposes of understanding psychopathology and psychotherapy as well as the development of higher needs, the crucial assumption in Maslow's theory is that the failure to satisfy earlier instinctual needs is the antecedent condition to the failure to develop the higher needs and psychological health. The implication is that if we could gratify all needs of everyone more profusely, everyone would be healthier and happier. It appears to be a kindly and reasonable proposition. However, at least two of the theorists discussed in earlier chapters disagree with this assertion, and there does seem to be some evidence to the contrary. Too much gratification, according to Freud, can lead to fixation, a prediction just the opposite of Maslow's. From Adler's point of view, too much indulgence, and protection can lead to a pampered style of life, a source of many difficulties. There is clearly evidence that overprotection, indulgence, and providing children with "too-easy" gratification does lead to a variety of problems of adjustment. Possibly Maslow would say that it was the wrong kind of gratification, but he fails to describe what is the right kind.

In summary, Maslow presents a rather general theory of motivation and personality development. He has rejected the study of lower animals as a reasonable basis for understanding human behavior. On the other hand, he has not provided us with many details of the processes which *do* govern human behavior, and his theories are stated in such form as to make empirical investigation extremely difficult. Maslow has also tried to emphasize the positive aspects of human behavior which he feels have been neglected in many other theories. He is not afraid to tackle such problems as happiness, love, conscience, and social responsibility. His is a theory directed towards explaining the uniqueness of the human being and the potential richness of his life. The practical value of the theory or its susceptibility to scientific study has yet to be demonstrated, and it is possible that many of Maslow's personal values have entered into the theory as statements of the facts of human nature. Perhaps the theory's greatest value lies in the attention it will bring to important aspects of human behavior which have been neglected by too many psychologists.

8

ROTTER'S SOCIAL LEARNING THEORY

The theories we have discussed thus far have all been based primarily upon the theorists' clinical experiences. As we pointed out earlier, many of the major constructs in these theories have proved difficult to operationalize. The lack of good operations for measuring constructs leads to difficulties in testing hypotheses and confusion in the interpretation of experimental results. One cannot state with any degree of confidence that repression of powerful id material leads to neurotic symptoms unless one can measure repression reliably, using operations which are generally considered to be valid indicators of what is meant by this term. Very often, however, when experimentally-oriented psychologists devise ways of measuring certain constructs that are used by clinicians, their work is viewed by those involved in clinical work as inaccurate and oversimplified. This conflict between those who insist upon experimentally verifiable hypotheses and those who believe that the objective study of clinical notions is trivial, unnecessary, or subject to distortion has continued for many years.

One result of this long-standing dilemma has been the development of "miniature" theories or empirically-derived approaches which focus upon a single personality variable (e.g., aggression, anxiety, altruism) which can be rigorously studied both in the laboratory and in natural settings. Some examples of this approach will be discussed in Chapter 10. A second outcome of the controversy has been the attempt on the part of some personality psychologists/clinicians to construct personality theories which take into account the relatively recent work done by experimental psychologists in the fields of learning and perception. Dollard and Miller (1950), for example, constructed a theory of personality which represents an attempt to wed a modern process theory, Hullian learning theory, with Freud's content theory. Mowrer (1950) has also attempted to apply learning theory to the problems of neurosis and psychotherapy. The learning model used by these psychologists stemmed primarily from the studies of subhuman species in highly controlled, relatively simple laboratory experiments. Social learning theory (Rotter, 1954), developed by the senior author and his colleagues, is based upon research with humans in relatively complex social situations as well as upon clinical experience derived from individual case studies.

BASIC ASSUMPTIONS

The first assumption of social learning theory is that the unit of investigation for the study of personality is the interaction of the individual and his meaningful environment. Personality is not viewed as a set of internal characteristics which the individual carries around with him from situation to situation, but rather as a set of potentials for responding to particular kinds of social situations. It follows from this principle that the study of personality is the study of learned behavior—that is, behavior that is modifiable and that changes with experiences in a variety of life situations. The understanding of personality requires a historical approach; the individual's behavior in the present is seen as influenced or shaped by the experiences he has had in his personal past.

Rotter, along with many other personality theorists, assumes that personality has unity. A person's experiences, his interactions with his environment, influence each other. The individual's new experiences are influenced by what he has learned in the past, and things that he has learned in the past are in turn changed by new experiences. Personality is thus seen as: (1) continuously changing, since the person is always undergoing new experiences, and (2) stable in certain respects, since his previous experiences affect new learning.

Another major assumption of social learning theory deals with the nature of motivation. Behavior as described by personality constructs is seen as goal directed. Rotter rejects drive reduction as a sufficient explanation for motivated behavior. In explaining complex human behavior, he suggests, it is necessary to define reinforcement more broadly than it is usually defined—as anything that leads to drive reduction. Rotter, therefore, uses the empirical law of effect in his theory. This law defines reinforcement as any action, condition, or event which affects the individual's movement toward a goal. Reinforcements that facilitate movement toward a goal (e.g., candy given to a child for good behavior, high marks given for excellence in schoolwork) are considered positive reinforcements. Reinforcing events that inhibit or frustrate such movement (e.g., taking away privileges from a child who misbehaves, giving poor grades for laziness in schoolwork) are considered negative reinforcements. A positive reinforcement is something which will increase the likelihood that a particular behavior will occur again under similar circumstances (e.g., that the child reinforced with candy for cooperating with a baby-sitter will continue to behave well when he's left with a baby-sitter again); a negative reinforcement is something which will decrease the likelihood that a particular behavior will occur in the future (e.g., the child sent to his room immediately after dinner because of bad behavior with a baby-sitter will be less likely to misbehave when left with the baby-sitter again).

BASIC CONSTRUCTS

Social learning theory is a more complex theory than most and requires the analysis of four kinds of variables in order to make a prediction about an individual's behavior. In contrast, some of the theories which we have discussed base their predictions on the identification of a single strong trait or internal characteristic of the person, or on the conflict between two equally strong traits or motivating forces.

Behavior Potential

The first of the four variables which comprise the basic predictive formula of the theory is *behavior potential* (BP). This refers to the potential for any given behavior to occur in a particular situation or set of situations as calculated in relation to any single reinforcement or set of reinforcements. For example, in academic testing situations (in which reinforcements are good grades, status among classmates, etc.), a student may rely on a number of possible behaviors, such as studying hard, cheating in order to get good grades, playing sick in order to get out of examinations, and so on. Each of these behaviors may be said to have a given potential for a particular individual, and one can talk about one behavior as more or less likely to occur than other behaviors. In any situation, the behavior potential may only be characterized as being stronger or weaker than some other behavior potentials.

The concept of behavior that is used here is a broad one. It includes any action of the individual that involves a response to some stimulus situation and that may be observed or measured either directly or indirectly. Behavior may thus consist of actual motor acts, cognitions, verbal behavior, nonverbal expressive behavior, emotional reactions, and so on. Many of the psychoanalytic or Adlerian defense mechanisms are describable as behaviors; for example, avoiding particular kinds of situations, blaming others for one's own mistakes, and displacing aggressive actions so that they are expressed toward safe objects.

Expectancy

The second major variable is the *expectancy* (E) construct. Expectancy is defined as the probability held by the individual that a particular reinforcement will occur as a function of a specific behavior on his part in a specific situation or situations. The emphasis placed on the concept of expectancy sets this theory apart from most others. Whether or not a behavior will occur is considered to be not only a function of the nature and importance of the reinforcement that the individual desires but also of the individual's anticipation or expectancy that he will be able to achieve this goal if he behaves in a particular way. Such expectations are determined by his previous experience and can be described quantitatively. Rotter contends that simply knowing how much an individual wants to reach a certain goal is not sufficient information for predicting his behavior. A student may want very badly to finish school and qualify himself for a well-paying job. But if his past experiences have led him to believe that no amount of studying will result in passing grades—if his expectancy for success in this situation is low—he is unlikely to study, despite his strong desire to graduate. A fellow student may share the same strong goals and, as a result of a different set of past experiences in school, have a high expectancy that studying will lead to academic success. In this instance, one could safely predict that the second student would be likely to study in order to obtain his goals. As you can see, the goals in these two cases are identical, but the expectancies differ, and as a result, the behavior of the two students is likely to differ.

There are several further points to be made concerning the concept of expectancy. According to the theory, expectancies are subjective in nature, and the person's subjective feelings about the probability of his being reinforced for some behavior may or may not coincide with the realistic probability. Clearly, some individuals' expectancies for success are low in situations where their actual probability of succeeding is, in fact, high. Similarly, people often anticipate success under circumstances in which a positive outcome is, in point of fact, quite unlikely to occur. Like Adler, Rotter stresses that it is not the situation *per se* which is important in predicting behavior, but rather the way in which a particular individual perceives that situation. A person may or may not be able to verbalize his expectancy in a given situation.

Expectancies are viewed as varying in generality. At one end of the continuum, one may talk about an individual's expectancy with regard to a very specific situation (E^1); for example, an individual's expectancy for success in a particular French class. At the most general level, one may use the concept of generalized expectancy (GE); for example, a person's expectancy for academic success in all his classes. A generalized expectancy is one which is held by the individual in a variety of situations. It is assumed to be the result of accumulated experiences which generalize from one situation to other situations which are viewed as similar in some respect. We shall further examine the generalized expectancy construct later in this chapter.

Reinforcement Value

The third major variable in social learning theory is that of *reinforcement value (RV)*. This refers to the degree of preference for any reinforcement to occur if the possibilities of their occurring were all equal. For example, most people would consistently choose to be paid ten dollars an hour for their work instead of one dollar an hour if it were only a matter of choice on their part, since the reinforcement value of ten dollars is greater than that of one dollar in our culture. Individuals differ in the degree to which they value various reinforcements. In a social situation such as a party, for example, a variety of reinforcements are potentially available to the partygoer, such as gaining status by trying to impress other people; finding a partner for sexual activity or to meet affectional needs; making contacts that will be useful in terms of financial gain; obtaining intellectual stimulation, and so on. Given all of these potentially available goals or reinforcements, people will differ in their preferences for pursuing any particular goal. Moreover, it can be readily demonstrated that, for both individuals and cultures, some degree of consistency or reliability exists in the degree to which any reinforcement is preferred by the individual or group.

One important characteristic of reinforcements is that they usually do not occur entirely independently of one another; the occurrence of one reinforcement may have expected consequences for future reinforcements. Rotter refers to reinforcement-reinforcement sequences, and suggests that people develop expectancies (E^2s) that a particular reinforcing event (e.g., good grades in school) will lead to other reinforcements (e.g., graduation), which will lead to still other reinforcements (e.g., a well-paying job), and so on. All of these expected future reinforcements contribute to the value of the present reinforcement. Thus, the value of obtaining good grades in school will be higher for a person who does indeed expect that the grades will be followed by a desirable job (plus security, ability to support a family, material rewards, etc.) than it will be for a person who does not expect that these future reinforcements will be a natural consequence of obtaining good grades (e.g., someone who expects that racial discrimination will prevent him from getting a good job regardless of his academic accomplishments).

In discussing expectancies, we predicted differences in behavior between two people who, in a given situation, had identically valued goals but who differed in their expectancies for success as a result of a particular behavior. One would also predict differences in behavior if these factors were reversed—that is, if the persons' expectancies were identical but they differed in the degree to which they valued a given reinforcement.

Psychological Situation

A major feature of social learning theory is the attention given explicitly to the role of the psychological situation of the individual. In contrast with theories which focus exclusively on internal states or characteristics, this view, because of its basic learning theory assumptions, emphasizes that a person learns through past experiences that some satisfactions are more likely to be obtained in certain situations than in others. Individual differences exist in the way in which situations are perceived.

Personality theories, until quite recently, have been characterized by their failure to deal analytically with the situations or contexts in which human beings are involved. Although we are aware that in animal studies changes in lighting, temperature, and so on, may result in considerably different behavior in trained animals, we have made little systematic progress in attempting to understand the behavior of people as a function of the objectively definable situations in which they find themselves. While social psychologists have focused their attention on situational variables and have tended to ignore individual differences, personality psychologists have tried to predict behavior as a function of internal characteristics (traits, drives, character fixations, and so on) and have ignored the effects of situational variables.

The *situation* (s), the fourth major variable in social learning theory, refers to the psychological situation or any part of the situation to which the individual is responding. The subjective reaction, the meanings the person himself gives to the situation, are important. The situation must also be describable in objective terms for scientific purposes. It is not enough to simply state that for each person a given situation may have different meanings; one must attempt to describe in some communicable way what it is that has different meanings for different people. In psychology, we often describe situations in terms of the kinds of reinforcements that are available or the kinds of behaviors that are generally considered appropriate in various situations. For example, we may discuss social, academic, competitive, evaluative, or achievement situations. When we do this, what we are saying is that certain cues in particular situations are more important than other cues. This provides a relatively objective definition in the sense that most people would attend to these specified cues rather than to others.

Predictive Formulas and the Concept of Psychological Needs

Rotter hypothesizes specific relationships among the four major variables in social learning theory. He suggests the following basic formula for the prediction of goal-directed behavior:

$$BP_{x,s_1R_a} = f(E_{x,R_as_1} \& RV_{a,s_1})$$

The formula may be read as follows: The potential for behavior x to occur in situation *l* in relation to reinforcement *a* is a function of the expectancy of the occurrence of reinforcement *a* following behavior x in situation *l* and the value of reinforcement *a* in situation *l*. This formula allows one to predict whether or not a specific behavior is likely to occur in a particular situation. For example, if one wished to predict how much a student will study for his final exam in mathematics, one would have to assess: (1) his expectancy that studying in this math course is likely to lead to his achieving a high grade, and (2) how much he values this particular reinforcement—how important to him is a high grade on this exam. His expectancy for success as a result of studying will have been influenced by his past experiences in this math course (E^1) and perhaps by experiences he has had in courses which were similar in content or level of difficulty (GE). The degree to which he values the reinforcement in question (a high grade) will depend upon the value he places upon reinforcements he expects to be associated with or to follow from his getting a high grade (e.g., respect or admiration from other people, a higher cumulative average which will allow him to enter a good graduate program, etc.). Methods to measure an individual's expectancy and reinforcement value in this situation could be readily devised in order to predict, with reasonable accuracy, how hard the student is likely to study for the examination.

The above formula is somewhat limited in application, for it deals only with the prediction of a specific behavior in relation to a single specific reinforcement. This focus on specifics is useful for testing hypotheses in highly controlled laboratory studies. Application of the theory in clinical settings requires a broader approach. Psychotherapists are not so much interested in predicting very specific instances of behavior; rather, they are concerned with the understanding and prediction of classes of behaviors, such as aggressive behaviors, defensive behaviors, and so on. Therefore, Rotter suggests the following formula which may be used for more general prediction:

$$NP = f(FM \& NV)$$

This formula states that the potential for the occurrence of a set of behaviors that lead to the satisfaction of some need (Need Potential) is a function of the expectancies that these behaviors will lead to these reinforcements (Freedom of Movement) and the value of these reinforcements (Need Value). Or, even more simply, need potential is a function of freedom of movement and need value. In this formula, the situational construct is implicit.

According to social learning theory, one's behavior is determined by one's goals. A person responds with those behaviors that he has learned will lead to the greatest satisfaction in a given situation. The goals or reinforcements sought by the person change as a result of experience. For example, an infant is at first satisfied by the mother's feeding him; then the presence of the mother in itself becomes pleasurable; then the child may strive to do things of which the mother approves, until finally, even in the absence of the mother, he will derive satisfaction from accomplishments once associated with her approval. Gradually, a set of motives, or needs, develops.

Rotter suggests that a need has three essential components. The first of these is a set of behaviors directed toward the same goal (or similar goals), such as the set of behaviors used by a person to get others to take care of him. The potential occurrence of these related behaviors is called *need potential*.

The second major component of a need is the set of expectancies that these related behaviors will lead to goals that a person values. An individual may have learned many ways of getting others to take care of him as a child, but at the present time he may have little expectation that they will lead to satisfaction. For example, crying will usually result in an infant's being helped and cared for, but a ten or twelve-year-old boy using the same technique may find himself being rejected by his father as a "sissy." The average level of the expectancies that the behaviors one has learned to rely upon to achieve certain satisfactions will actually lead to those satisfactions is referred to as *freedom of movement*.

The third component of needs is the value, *need value*, attached to the goals themselves—that is, the degree to which an individual prefers one set of satisfactions to another set. For example, given a situation in which both kinds of satisfactions are available, one person may prefer to do something for which others will admire him (recognition need), while another person may prefer to do something which will make others like him (love and affection need).

The content of social learning theory consists of a number of empirically determined needs—that is, groups of behaviors which are related in the sense that they lead to the same or similar reinforcements. For illustrative purposes, six very broad needs are listed below with their definitions. This list represents an attempt to include most kinds of learned psychological behavior. But these terms are so broad that they permit only limited prediction, and more specific concepts are necessary for the purpose of accurate prediction. For example, the need for recognition and status can be broken down and discussed in terms of specific kinds of situations; such as the need for recognition and status in social activities, occupational pursuits, intellectual activities, athletic situations, and so on.

(1) *Recognition-status:* The need to excel, to be considered competent, good, or better than others in school, occupation, profession, athletics,

social position, physical appeal, or play; that is, the need to obtain a high position on a socially valued competitive scale.

(2) *Dominance:* The need to control the actions of other people, including family and friends; to be in a position of power, to have others follow one's own ideas and desires.

(3) *Independence:* The need to make one's own decisions, rely on oneself, to develop the skill necessary to obtain satisfaction and reach goals without the help of others.

(4) *Protection-dependency:* The need to have another person or persons prevent frustration, provide protection and security, and help one to obtain other desired goals.

(5) *Love and affection:* The need for acceptance and liking by other people, to have their warm regard, interest, concern, and devotion.

(6) *Physical comfort:* The need for physical satisfactions that have become associated with security and a state of well-being, the avoidance of pain, and the desire for bodily pleasures.

LOW FREEDOM OF MOVEMENT AND HIGH NEED VALUE

An important part of social learning theory is its specific hypotheses regarding the behavior of an individual with low freedom of movement and high need value for a particular class of satisfaction; for example, the young person who places a high value on obtaining love and affection from someone of the opposite sex, but who has very low expectations for success in this area. Such an individual is likely to learn behaviors which serve to avoid the failure or punishments that he anticipates in certain situations and may attempt to achieve his goals on an "irreal" (fantasy) level. Trying to avoid anticipated punishment or failure, he may avoid particular situations physically or by repression, or he may attempt to obtain satisfaction by means of rationalization, fantasy, or symbolic means. For example, the boy who fears rejection from females may avoid parties or other situations in which he might experience such rejection; he might repress or actively suppress sexual thoughts; he might try to convince himself that he isn't really interested in girls at this time because of pressing academic concerns; or he might, to some extent, withdraw into a fantasy world in which he receives all the love and affection he desires.

In social learning theory, the great variety of behaviors commonly regarded as defenses or psychopathological symptoms are referred to as *avoidance* and *irreal* behaviors. These behaviors often start a "vicious cycle" of psychological difficulties and lead to both immediate and delayed additional negative reinforcements. Thus, the person who, because he expects failure, comes to rely on defensive behaviors or symptomatic behaviors (e.g., obsessive thoughts, compulsive rituals, constant bodily complaints, narrowing the field of attention and therefore "missing" much of what is going on around him, etc.), will often receive further negative feedback from others, which increases his expectancy for failure still more and may lead to even more serious problems. As symptoms or maladaptive behaviors accumulate in this way, efforts directed toward constructive behavior or problem solution may be seriously hampered. Thus, according to this theory, many of the psychological problems experienced by persons who might be seen in psychotherapy arise as a result of their experiencing low freedom of movement in relation to valued goals.

An individual's low freedom of movement might have several possible origins, according to Rotter. For example, low freedom of movement may result from the person's lack of knowledge or ability to learn the behaviors necessary for reaching his goals. A major problem for some people who fear rejection from the opposite sex is a deficit of social skills necessary for getting to know another person. Secondly, low freedom of movement may be related to the nature of the goal itself; the goal may be inappropriate (e.g., the desire on the part of an adult to have others take care of him and take responsibility for his actions) or it may be a goal which is set so high that it is realistically unobtainable. A third possible origin of a condition of low freedom of movement lies in the generalization of expectancies from one area of life to other areas. For example, a person who has had negative experiences in athletic and academic situations, and who considers himself a failure as a result, may generalize his low expectancies for success to other areas, such as social activities; thus, without really testing himself in the social arena, he expects rejection and tends to avoid potentially painful social encounters. Mistaken evaluation of present circumstances because of early experiences in certain need areas is another source of low freedom of movement. For example, a boy whose older brother was always considered better looking may grow up thinking of himself as unattractive when, in fact, others consider him quite good looking. A person's image of himself as unattractive, clumsy, unintelligent, or uninteresting may be carried into adulthood despite the fact that other people no longer react negatively with regard to such attributes. In summary, the difficulty experienced by the low-freedom-of-movement individual may be a problem of inadequate or inappropriate behaviors or skills, "erroneous" expectancies, or unrealistic goals. In the psychotherapy section below, we shall discuss techniques designed to increase a person's freedom of movement, having first determined whether the major problem lies in the area of behaviors, and/or expectancies, and/or goals.

MINIMAL GOAL LEVEL

One important aspect of low freedom of movement relates to the concept of *minimal goal level*. In any given situation, the possible outcomes of behavior can be ordered on a scale from a very strong positive reinforcement (or reward) to a very strong negative reinforcement (or punishment). The theoretical point at which, in this ordering, the outcome changes from positive to negative is called the minimal goal level. Such a concept can be applied either to a series of goals of the same class (e.g., school grades: A, B, C, D, etc.) or to any combination of outcomes possible in a given situation or set of situations. Even though from the point of view of others he often appears to succeed, a person may have low freedom of movement because his reinforcements are usually below his own (high) minimal goal level. An example of high minimal goals is the student who is disappointed and unhappy because he received one B grade along with three A's. Setting exceedingly high goals for oneself only leads to difficulties if one generally fails to reach them. (The student who finds any grade lower than an A unacceptable but who usually succeeds in getting straight A's in his courses has no problem because he can, if he works hard, achieve his goals.) Another example of high minimal goal level is the person with very high goals for social status who is ashamed to be seen with any person of the opposite sex who is not well known on campus as an athlete, a student activist leader, a gifted artist, or scholar. Such internalized high minimal goals are frequently involved in problems of low freedom of movement. It should be emphasized that the goals in question may be of any kind: moral, ethical, academic, sexual, affectional, dominating, dependent, and so on. The lowering of unrealistically high goals in any of these areas is likely to lead to the individual's obtaining greater satisfactions and increased self-confidence or expectancies for success. For this reason, a person's minimal goal levels may be a prime focus of attention in psychotherapy.

GENERALIZED EXPECTANCIES: PROBLEM-SOLVING SKILLS

Another area of content in social learning theory concerns the individual's problem-solving skills. Needs are only one important index of individual differences. People may differ in their attitudes toward different kinds of people and social issues (social attitudes) and in the ways in which they respond to strong reinforcement or their anticipation of strong reinforcement (emotional behavior). In addition, individuals seem to differ in the ways in which they approach a variety of different situations from a problem-solving point of view.

Rotter suggests that it is useful to talk about generalized expectancies that certain kinds of behaviors are likely to lead to problem solution across a number of different kinds of situations. Such expectancies or attitudes (related to intellectual tasks) have been described as higher-level learning skills by Harry Harlow. The notion of generalized expectancies, however, is a broader concept in that such expectancies are seen as operating in social situations as well as in intellectual problem-solving situations. Several generalized expectancies of this type have been studied experimentally.

People differ in their reactions to situations in which behavior directed toward some goal is blocked. One constructive strategy for solving such a problem is to look for alternative ways of achieving the desired goal. If this strategy proves to be an effective one in a particular kind of situation (for example, in an academic situation), it may generalize to other situations (social, moral, occupational); the person may then be said to have a generalized expectancy that a particular kind of behavior, *looking for alternative solutions,* will lead to maximum satisfaction or problem solution in many situations.

Another generalized expectancy is referred to as *internal versus external control of reinforcement.* People are known to differ in their belief that what happens to them is the result of their own behaviors and attributes (internal control) versus the result of luck, fate, chance, or powerful others (external control). Clearly, persons who believe or expect that they can control their own destinies will behave differently, in many situations, than those who expect that their outcomes are controlled by other people or determined by luck.

Another generalized expectancy which has implications for behavior across a variety of situations concerns *interpersonal trust.* There is evidence that there are generalized differences in the degree to which people believe others and feel that they can be relied upon to tell the truth and do what they say they will do. Such generalized expectancies that others can or cannot be trusted are likely to affect people's behavior in school, marriage, psychotherapy, and virtually every kind of social interaction.

Generalized expectancies for internal-external control (Rotter, 1966) and interpersonal trust (Rotter, 1971) have been studied extensively and have proved useful for the prediction of a wide variety of behaviors. Some of these studies will be described in Chapter 10. In social learning theory, such concepts are considered central issues in psychotherapy and other situations which involve learning constructive ways of dealing with life's problems.

PSYCHOTHERAPY

Rotter maintains that when freedom of movement is low and need value high—in other words, when an individual has a low expectation of obtaining certain gratifications which he strongly desires—then defensive or maladaptive behavior frequently arises. Instead of learning how to achieve his goals, the person learns how to avoid, or defend himself against, failure and the frustration of not achieving these goals; or he may attempt to reach the goals by irreal means. For a given person, the primary source of difficulty may lie in lack of necessary skills or behaviors, inappropriate or unrealistic nature of goals, or "erroneous" expectancies. The focus of change in psychotherapy is determined by the clinician's understanding of the particular problem area or areas contributing to the condition of low freedom of movement. The general goal of psychotherapy is to increase the patient's freedom of movement, thereby increasing his satisfactions in life and reducing his reliance upon defensive or avoidant behaviors.

In order to increase a patient's freedom of movement for goals which he values highly, the therapist may focus upon changing the importance of the goals themselves. This might be necessary for a person who has two or more highly valued goals which conflict with each other in such a way that the satisfaction of one need involves the frustration of the other. An example might be the person who desires to meet his needs for masculinity and dependency in the same situation. Another kind of goal problem exists when a person's goals are inappropriate or destructive in that they usually lead to failure or negative reinforcements—for example, the person whose desire to dominate and control others leads to conflicts with others' needs and results in both immediate and delayed punishments. A third kind of goal problem concerns the patient with unrealistically high minimal goals in a given need area, such as a man who regards any indication of fear in himself as proof that he is not sufficiently masculine and who consequently goes to extreme lengths to avoid any "proof" of his lack of masculinity.

As noted above, it is sometimes the case that although a patient's goals are realistic and appropriate for his social group and although his expectancies are accurately based on experiences in present situations, his problem may lie in his having learned inadequate ways of achieving his goals. Rotter, like Adler, suggests that the most efficient way for the psychotherapist to deal with this kind of problem is to actively suggest new behaviors for the patient to try out. The clinician may try to teach the patient how to search for alternative ways of reaching goals. This emphasis on the acquisition of new and more effective behaviors distinguishes the social learning theory approach from other kinds of psychotherapy which are based on the assumption that once a person is free from internal conflict and understands himself better, he will automatically be able to find healthier ways of achieving his goals. Insight into one's problems may be very useful but does not always lead to actual changes in a person's behavior.

Low expectancies for success with regard to a certain need area may be "erroneous" in the sense that they may be (1) based on past experiences (e.g., the gawky adolescent who continues to feel physically awkward as an adult, although others no longer perceive him in this way), or (2) generalized from other need areas (e.g., the person who, because he doesn't excel in academic activities, feels that he is probably not good at anything). A more realistic appraisal of the person's characteristics and abilities is necessary if such mistaken expectancies are to change. The therapist may provide such feedback himself or may suggest that the patient try a group therapy situation in which the feedback he receives from other members of the group might result in changed expectancies.

In predicting behavior, social learning theorists stress the importance of the psychological situation in addition to internal states. The individual who is dominating and inconsiderate at work may be submissive and affectionate when he is at home with his family. The child who has learned that he can "get away with anything" at home may be quite docile and cooperative at school, once he has learned that he will be punished for disruptive behavior in that setting. Similarly, the child who is cooperative and giving in the warm, affectionate atmosphere of the home may be sullen and hostile in a school situation in which he feels that he is being ignored or treated unfairly. From this point of view, personality is not merely composed of characteristics within the individual; rather, it is a potential to respond in a given way to a given situation.

Two implications of emphasizing the importance of the psychological situation in determining behavior are: (1) that the psychotherapist should attempt to develop the patient's ability to discriminate among different situations and to understand other people's needs and reactions, and (2) that he or she should make use of environmental control — that is, try to effect changes in the person's surroundings as a vehicle for behavior change. Some examples of the need for these therapeutic strategies might prove useful.

Many people come into therapy and express bewilderment concerning the causes for their failures or the reasons for other people's negative reactions toward them. Often the problem lies in their inability to discriminate among situations or people. The man who has enjoyed great social success as a result of his casual style and ability to tell jokes at the drop of a hat may behave in this way during job interviews and experience frequent rejection without understanding that his behavior, while entirely appropriate in one kind of situation, is very inappropriate in another kind of situation. A man whose mother reacts approvingly when he is oversolicitous and fusses over her may be rejected by other women who view this behavior as excessive and somewhat annoying. Psychotherapy, in cases such as these, would be aimed at increasing the patients' awareness of the cues that distinguish one kind of situation from another or one kind of person from another.

Environmental treatment may take many forms. Rotter agrees with Adler in emphasizing the need for involving significant adults (parents, teachers, etc.) when dealing with children's problems. Adults' attitudes and behaviors with regard to a child's difficulties are often the result of lack of knowledge about some of the child's characteristics or lack of understanding of the ways in which their behavior affects the child's behavior. But, with the clinician's help, it is often possible for parents and teachers to change their attitudes and behaviors in ways which are helpful in improving the child's adjustment and increasing his satisfactions.

In many cases, however, the parents' behavior is a reflection of their own serious maladjustment, and more thorough, long-term treatment is necessary before they can make changes. Such treatment may begin by centering on the child's problem, but it usually shifts to the parents and their own problems. For example, when parents' behavior toward a child is a result of their overly strong needs to dominate and control, or when one or both parents seek from the child the love they cannot obtain from a disinterested or punitive marital partner, or when parents try to obtain, through their offspring, the status and recognition they failed to obtain themselves, then changes in the parents themselves must occur before they can be expected to react differently to their children's difficulties.

The environmental treatment of adults may involve a suggested change in a patient's job, academic situation, living conditions, and so on. Very often it is advisable to treat marital partners or other people who are closely associated with the patient. The assumption here is that the problems that a person experiences are usually not all "in his head" but are significantly affected by the situations in which he finds himself in his daily life.

There are several general characteristics of the application of social learning theory to psychotherapy. One such characteristic is the flexibility required of the therapist. Since patients enter therapy with different motives and different past experiences, it is assumed that the conditions for optimal learning will vary from patient to patient. Therefore, no single technique can be applied to all cases. Environmental treatment, behavior therapy techniques, various kinds of interpretations, direct or indirect suggestions, supportive therapy with minimal interpretation — all of these may be used singly or in combination.

Another major characteristic of social learning theory is its problem-solving orientation toward the patient's difficulties. The theory emphasizes the development of problem-solving skills on the part of the patient, such as looking for alternative ways of reaching goals, analyzing the consequences of behavior, understanding the motives of others, and trying to analyze how situations differ from one another. The goal of therapy is not only to help the person solve his immediate problems, but to provide him with skills which will be useful to him in meeting life's difficulties in the future.

Psychotherapy is viewed by Rotter as a learning process. Not only are there inadequate behaviors and attitudes to be weakened or eliminated, but also more satisfying and constructive alternatives to be learned. As a result, the therapist is likely, in most cases, to play a highly active role. He is active in making interpretations, in directly reinforcing or rewarding particular kinds of behavior, and in suggesting alternative courses of action or ways of looking at people or events.

CHARACTERISTIC RESEARCH

It was pointed out earlier in this chapter that a mistaken expectancy for failure may result from experiences of frustration in one area of life which generalize to other areas. For example, a child who learns that he cannot do well in athletic activities because of some physical difficulty may generalize these feelings of inadequacy to other areas and feel that because he cannot play as well as other children, others don't like him. Another example would be that of a child who does poorly in school and feels, because he cannot achieve grades that his parents and teachers find acceptable, that other children will reject him because he is a "dummy."

That such generalizations do occur is demonstrated in a study by Vaughn Crandall (1955). Crandall developed a method of measuring subjects' freedom of movement on the basis of stories they told about pictures of the thematic apperception type (see Chapter 8). He developed two equivalent sets of nine pictures each in order to measure freedom of movement in three need areas. Each need area was represented by three pictures. The three need areas represented were: (1) recognition for physical skill (athletic coordination); (2) recognition for academic skill; and (3) love and affection from the opposite sex.

Crandall gave one set of pictures to a group of thirty male subjects and asked them to make up stories. Then he asked the subjects to perform a series of difficult, if not impossible, coordination tasks at which they all failed. After this failure experience he gave them the second series of nine pictures in order to measure changes in freedom of movement that took place in all three need areas when the subjects were frustrated only in the need area of recognition for athletic skills. Judges rated all stories for freedom of movement on a scale of zero to seven. A control group of thirty-six subjects did not have the failure experience following the first series of pictures. Instead, they spent an equivalent amount of time in "neutral" activity, and then told stories to the second set of pictures. Figure 1 shows the results of the study.

The results indicate differing degrees of decreases in freedom of movement for the frustrated group as compared with the control group. Subjects who had experienced frustration in the athletic coordination task show increased expectancy for failure (lower freedom of movement) in the area of recognition for physical skills. Freedom of movement also decreased significantly, but not as much, in the somewhat related area of recognition for academic skills. Freedom of movement decreased still less in the more unrelated area of gratification from peers of the opposite

FIGURE 1   DIFFERENCE IN THE AMOUNT OF LOWERING OF FREEDOM OF MOVEMENT IN CRANDALL'S EXPERIMENTAL SUBJECTS COMPARED TO HIS CONTROL SUBJECTS

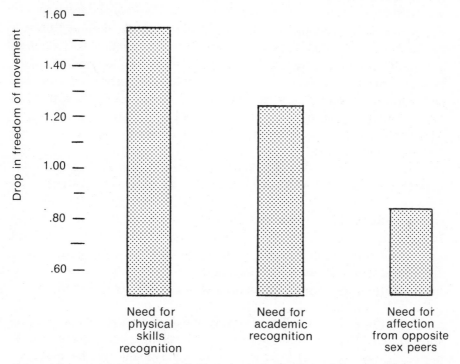

From data reported by Crandall, V. J. An investigation of the specificity of reinforcement of induced frustration. *Journal of Social Psychology*, 1955, **41,** 311–318. Julian B. Rotter, *Clinical Psychology*, © 1964, page 84. Reprinted by permission of Prentice-Hall, Inc., Englewood Cliffs, New Jersey.

sex. Since the frustrating failure occurred only in the area of physical skills, this study demonstrates how expectancies for failure may generalize from one need area to others.

MAJOR CONTRIBUTIONS

A major value of social learning theory lies in the systematic nature of the theory and its emphasis upon operationalizing problems in the field of personality. Constructs and hypothesized relationships among constructs are stated in such a way as to allow for controlled investigation. As a result of this emphasis, the theory has stimulated research in a variety of areas: learning theory, personality development, social psychology, psychopathology, psychotherapy, and so on (Rotter, Chance, & Phares, 1972).

The theory has also proved useful in the further development of both the theory and methodology of personality measurement (see Chapter 10). While more empirical data is needed (for the development of useful content categories of behaviors, reinforcements, expectancies, and psychological situations) before the theory can be systematically applied to psychotherapy situations, it has already had some influence upon psychotherapists who favor a learning approach emphasizing both cognitive and behavioral change.

SUMMARY AND ANALYSIS OF SOCIAL LEARNING THEORY

Social learning theory represents an explicit attempt to systematize the study of personality. Compared with many other personality theories it is *relatively* well systematized. Basic assumptions are explicitly stated, all of the constructs are linked together, and most of the constructs and relationships are anchored by antecedent and consequent conditions.

Some psychologists might criticize the deliberate attempt to exclude constructs which cannot be operationalized or linked to the existing constructs of the theory as a limitation favoring systematization over description of the "true nature of man." One might ask, for example, how it is possible to build a theory of personality without concepts such as "emotions" and "anxiety." Social learning theory provides instead constructs such as low freedom of movement or expectancy for punishment and high freedom of movement or expectancy for gratification, as well as concepts dealing with positive and negative reinforcement and their consequences. Many of the psychological characteristics of "emotions," as described by others, are conceptualized here as behaviors having a potential of occurrence in various situations. It is a question still to be decided whether these constructs can serve to predict behavior as well or better than the older and more familiar constructs of emotions and anxiety viewed as special internal states.

Social learning theory is primarily a process theory, but it does have content categories which are systematically related to the theory. While Rotter suggests a number of psychological needs which seem to be important for people in our society, the list is not meant to provide a complete set of categories. Likewise, it is anticipated that future research will lead to the discovery of other generalized expectancies or higher-level learning skills that will be useful in understanding and predicting behavior. In the clinical application of social learning theory, the psychotherapist must use content categories based on his common sense and previous experience, until such time that sufficient empirical data have been collected to provide him with the most efficient set of categories found to be useful within a particular culture or subculture.

What is most needed in terms of content is a system of classification of social situations. Threatening versus nonthreatening situations, male versus female social objects, high- versus low-reward situations, and so on have been used by psychologists as broad categories; but full prediction of complex social behavior requires much more extensive study of the nature of psychological situations in any given subculture.

According to social learning theory, psychological behavior is learned behavior, and the theory contains no assumptions regarding genetic or constitutional determinants of behavior.

The use of the empirical law of effect provides the motivational basis for social learning theory. The theory is extremely flexible in that its four major constructs—behavior potential (need potential), expectancy (freedom of movement), reinforcement value (need value), and situation—may be dealt with on whatever level of generality is necessary for a particular purpose. All of these concepts can be readily measured by techniques logically consistent with the theory. Prediction of specific behaviors in specific situations and prediction of more general classes of behaviors in a set of related situations are equally feasible using the basic predictive formulas.

Prediction is based on the nature of the given situation in which the individual is participating as well as on his past experience. While both internal and situational characteristics are seen as equally important in understanding behavior, Rotter places greater emphasis upon the situation than do most other personality theorists.

While behavior may be viewed as relatively stable, since past experience plays a vital role in determining present behavior and serves to screen the individual's perception of present events, social learning theory includes no concept of fixation. Any significant new experience or set of experiences may lead to changes in personality or behavior, and such changes may occur with or without psychotherapy or other kinds of experiences aimed at change.

In summary, social learning theory is a well-systematized theory based on a model of human learning and placing great emphasis on social motivation. Its basic constructs of behavior potential, expectancy, and reinforcement value integrate two major orientations in psychology, the cognitive approach, and the stimulus-response or reinforcement approach. The theory was developed in such a way that all its constructs could be measured and the validity of its assumptions and hypotheses could be assessed. The content part of the theory, which specifies the parameters of individual differences and classifies situations, is only partially developed. At this point social learning theory is as much a way of thinking about and analyzing problems in personality as it is a source of answers to these problems.

9

Measuring Personality

In the previous chapters we have described some selected personality theories. There are many more, each with its own set of propositions or hypotheses, its own terms and language. How is anyone to know which of these theories is correct or is the most useful in understanding human beings? Which theory is more useful in solving such practical problems as how to help maladjusted people change, how to select the best people to be kindergarten teachers, or how to raise one's children?

It is doubtful that intuitive opinions or verbal arguments would lead to any agreement or feeling of certainty among reasonable people. The authors of these theories all have their own anecdotes, their own reasons, and their own way of viewing things, and they have honestly arrived at very different opinions regarding the nature of personality. The fact that there are so many theories is an indication that there are not enough objective data which everyone must accept or data for which the implications are sufficiently clear that they can be applied unequivocally to supporting one theory and challenging another.

To make progress in this field, we need to produce such data or information, and to do this, we need to produce methods of measuring the constructs which are used in personality theories. For example, if we want to find out whether or not some people are more aggressive because they have had more frustration than others, or because they were fixated by trauma at an early stage of development, or because they have learned to be aggressive by modeling the aggressive behaviors of people around them, then we need to provide ways of measuring overt aggression. Without measurement, there is no scientific way of testing hypotheses or making advances in knowledge.

PURPOSES OF PERSONALITY MEASUREMENT

Testing hypotheses is not the only reason for wanting to measure personality constructs. The study of personality may be regarded as a basic area in psychology, but it has many important applications. One of these is *selection;* just as we may use tests of intelligence or achievement to select people for graduate school or for job training as a mechanic, we need tests of personality to select people who will be good in particular kinds of jobs. It seems apparent that if we could produce valid, useful ways of measuring certain personality characteristics, we could do better in selecting people as elementary-school teachers, as psychotherapists, as salespersons, and so on. Such tests, from the point of view of the employer, may lead to increases in the quality and efficiency of work. Tests also may be used to advise people who wish to go into a particular field — to help them to determine whether they would be well suited for it and whether they are likely to be successful and happy with that kind of work. The use of personality tests for selection purposes in industry has often been criticized, frequently with justification. Sometimes such testing is criticized because the tests are really not valid and sometimes because they are not properly used. But the ethical use of good instruments could be beneficial both to society and to the individuals concerned.

Another application of personality measurement is in the practice of clinical psychology. The measurement of various kinds of problems of adjustment and personal characteristics is important for the treatment of maladjusted or unhappy individuals who are not achieving sufficient satisfaction in their lives. When such measurement is properly applied, it is usually for the purpose of aiding in their treatment. That is, the clinician is interested in making predictions about the specific individual, predictions which will lead to decisions regarding his treatment. Should he be hospitalized or not? What kind of a therapist would work best with him? What method of therapy is best suited to his case? What personality characteristics underlie his apparent or overt symptoms? Many questions of adjustment involve people who are not necessarily more maladjusted than the average person. For example: How effectively will a school child learn from a teaching machine in contrast to having a teacher present material to him? What kind of school or classroom atmosphere would be most conducive to learning for different kinds of school

children? How well will two individuals who have no previous knowledge of each other get along together as freshman roommates in college?

In summary, personality measurement is necessary and important for
three kinds of problems: (1) to test hypotheses and theories of personality—that is, for theoretical purposes, (2) to help in problems of selecting
people who will be more successful and happier in particular kinds of
work, and (3) to make clinical predictions about an individual's future
behavior. How these different purposes affect the kinds of instruments
that are developed will be discussed later in this chapter.

RELIABILITY AND VALIDITY

Before a trained psychologist would use a personality measure to test a
hypothesis or to assess an individual's characteristics, he would want to
know something about the reliability and validity of the instrument. *Reliability* refers to the reproducibility or consistency of the measurement.
For example, if the measure is a rating, we want to know whether someone else making the same rating with the same information would arrive
at the same or a similar score. If a subject took a test on one day, would
he be likely to obtain the same score a week later? If two people making
ratings or two forms of the same test produced very different measurements, we would say that the method used did not provide consistent
scores. If a measurement is not reliable, then we could not expect that if
we duplicated an experiment or tried to measure a trait of some person a
second time that we would obtain the same results.

There are three kinds of reliability that psychologists study. The first
of these is called *internal consistency*. In this kind of reliability the psychologist is interested in whether or not the different parts or items of a
test are all measuring the same thing. To determine internal consistency
the typical practice is to divide the test in half and to see whether the
two halves are closely related or unrelated. Tests can be divided in half
by matching items or stimuli, or by taking alternate items, or by comparing the first half with the second half.

Another form of reliability is often treated as the same but is actually
quite different. It is called *test-retest* reliability and is concerned with
the stability over time of what is being measured. In this case, one is interested in whether the trait or characteristic being measured fluctuates
from time to time. If fluctuations are large, then conclusions drawn
about what someone does at the particular time that he is given the test
are not applicable at a later time. Reliability or consistency over time is

often difficult to estimate because giving the same test the second time or administering an alternate form which is much like the first test provides a different psychological situation, since the subject is familiar with the items; he may or may not remember how he responded before, and he may have discussed the test items with other people in the meantime. In some tests which call for imaginative productions, he may choose on the second time to give different responses in order to decrease the boredom of taking the test a second time. As a consequence, test-retest reliability is often not a meaningful measure.

The third kind of reliability, *interrater* reliability, is of special importance in personality measurement. The ratings of judges are used in behavioral observation techniques, interviews, and projective techniques. Since this rating is a subjective judgment of someone observing or analyzing the responses of a subject, it is important to know whether these judgments are consistent. If two judges arrived at very different ratings of subjects' associations to a standard set of pictures, the interpretation of the results of the study would depend upon which judge's ratings were used. Unless the judges agree, one can hardly put any faith in conclusions made from the studies using instruments involving subjective judgment. When a test score depends on subjective judgment, it is necessary to have clear-cut definitions of what is being measured and carefully constructed manuals in order to develop a reliable instrument.

Validity refers to the degree to which a measuring instrument provides or produces an accurate measure of the characteristic or trait it is purported to measure. A test could be highly reliable but not a true measure of what it is supposed to be measuring. For example, one could try to devise an instrument which measured honesty and include items such as, "I am more honest than other people." The response which an individual gave might be consistent within the test and over time but still not be true and, therefore, not useful in predicting how honest he might be in other situations. In some cases the word "utility" describes the validity of an instrument better than the word "accuracy." For example, one might be able to use a particular test to predict the potential for delinquency and yet not be sure of the specific variables which are involved or are being measured by the instrument that is used.

There are various kinds of validity or utility and the methods of establishing the validity of a test are quite complex. Numerous books have been written on the methodology of establishing test validity. While we will not discuss these methods here, it should be noted that tests are not either valid or invalid, good or bad; rather, they can be said to have a particular degree of validity for a particular purpose. A test may be valid for one purpose but not for another. For example, a measure of trusting behavior may predict better than chance whether children in school will trust their teacher, and for that purpose it would be valid; but the same measure might not predict whether children will trust each other, and it would, therefore, be invalid for that purpose. It might be the case that a single, well-constructed test would be able to predict both, or it might be that trust of teachers is unrelated to trust of peers. The conceptualization of the nature of trusting behavior is extremely important in determining whether one general measure or two specific measures would be more appropriate and useful for prediction.

PROBLEMS OF PERSONALITY MEASUREMENT

While it is clear enough that good measures of personality can be extremely useful, it is not a simple matter to produce such measures. For example, it is much more difficult to devise a measure to tell us how dependent someone is than to determine how well he reads or how extensive his vocabulary is. To begin with, we have to discover whether, in the population we are studying, the trait or characteristic we wish to measure is *generalized*. It is possible that people may be dependent on parents but not upon friends, or upon members of the same sex but not members of the opposite sex, or perhaps just dependent upon one person and not dependent upon others. Not only may the objects of his dependency vary, but the situations in which he is dependent may vary. A particular person may behave very dependently when studying for examinations but not in social situations, or he may depend upon others for reassurance in regard to what is acceptable behavior in social situations but be a leader in athletic situations. Perhaps, what we are really interested in measuring is not dependency but a related variable such as conformity. This discussion is meant to illustrate that, in the field of personality, before we can even start the measurement process, there is a problem in determining conceptually what the characteristic is that we wish to measure, how generalized it is, and how useful a measure is likely to be after we have devised it.

Of course, the correct or most useful way to conceptualize what we observe is a problem in all sciences. Whether this problem is more complex in the field of personality may or may not be the case. However, it is important to stress the idea that the development of adequate measures or ways of assessing personality cannot be divorced from the conceptualization of the nature of the constructs to be measured. Some tests of personality are doomed to failure simply because the characteristics to be measured are badly conceptualized.

Assuming that we do have a good construct and a reasonably accurate understanding of how general or how specific it is, and assuming that the purposes for which we want to use the measure are clear, there are still specific problems to be dealt with in devising a test. In fact, a whole area of specialization has grown up specifically around construction and validation of personality tests. While psychologists have developed many ingenious ways of getting around or trying to partially solve some of the problems, there is still a long way to go before we will be able to make highly accurate predictions about the behavior of specific individuals from personality tests. We will discuss some of these problems of measurement under the three headings of (1) the motivation of the subject, (2) the psychological situation of testing, and (3) logical difficulties in operationalizing particular concepts.

In taking a personality test, it is clear that subjects may differ considerably in their goals or motivation. If we were testing for knowledge of vocabulary, there might be little reason for the subject to give an incorrect answer when he knew the correct one. However, if we wanted to measure how important it was to this subject to get good grades, there are some circumstances in which he might choose not to give us an accurate answer. He might consciously dissimulate for reasons of his own, or his response might be inaccurate because of motivations which he was not aware of. The tester's goal is usually to get as accurate an answer as possible from the subject. A subject, however, may have many goals, and his goals do not always correspond with those of the test administrator. The subject's goal may be to give as good an impression as possible in order to obtain the job he is applying for, or to avoid criticism, or to cover up a deficiency, and so on. A subject who really cared a great deal about grades might say he did not care very much because the attitude of caring was unpopular with his friends. Another subject who cared very little might say that he cared a great deal because he thought that such a response would affect his teacher in a positive manner. Even if the examiner were not his teacher, he might feel that it is always good to be on the safe side because one never knows who might see one's test results. Still another subject might care a great deal about his grades but feel considerable hostility toward the test examiner (e.g., because the examiner's manner was brusque, or because the subject feels he has been pressured into taking the test, etc), and he may respond inaccurately as an expression of his hostility or anger. Because the motivations of subjects can be so different and frequently cannot be controlled or known by the examiner, personality tests often are limited in their utility.

A second source of testing problems related to these motivational differences is the effect of different kinds of situations. The subject in an experiment run by his former instructor may respond in a way which he feels would please his instructor, but he may respond quite differently in an experiment run by an experimenter whom he does not know. He might take a given test seriously in an experimental situation in a classroom filled with strangers and casual acquaintances, but make a joke out of the same test administered in a dormitory with his friends also serving as subjects. The subject may respond differently if he believes his test responses are going to be read by people he knows or by no one he knows, and he may respond differently to a female examiner than he does to a male. Presumably, the purpose for which he is taking the test will produce different kinds of responses. Whether he is a subject for an experiment, an individual seeking help in a clinic, or an applicant for a job will certainly affect what he says about himself. The fact that the testing situation will affect responses also creates a problem in prediction, because one has to know whether the situation where prediction is desired is similar to the situation in which the testing is done. As we have pointed out in our discussion of social learning theory, the psychological situation is a strong determinant of behavior.

The third set of problems revolves around logical difficulties in operationalizing or measuring particular kinds of constructs. Suppose one were to try to devise a measure of repressed hostility. The test constructor could not ask subjects whether or not they have repressed hostility, because if it is repressed they would not be aware of it. If we assume that people with repressed hostility lean over backwards to deny any hostility, we would not know whether people who respond with such denials are in fact repressed, or simply extremely low on hostility, or responding in that particular fashion because they think it is the desirable or correct thing to say. Yet, repressed hostility might still be a good construct and worth measuring.

Some constructs, however, are difficult to measure simply because it is not logically clear how people who are high or low on the variable are supposed to behave. These are bad constructs. For example, the notion of self-actualization is appealing and sounds, intuitively, as though it might be an important way of looking upon human behavior. But how does one know if somebody else is self-actualizing? Would he act like a saint or a rogue? Would he be characterized by high achievement or by devoting himself to his personal hobbies? Would he extend himself for others and be universally liked, or would he mainly be interested in his own satisfactions so that others would be indifferent to him? The difficulty does not lie merely in the process of measurement but in the lack of clarity of the concept itself. Self-actualization may be too vague a construct to be adequately measured.

Other concepts may be so broad that adequate measurement is extremely difficult. For example, psychoanalysts speak about the ego functions as those which are related to self-preservation and contact with reality. Frequently, they use the terms *strong ego* and *weak ego* in describing particular individuals. While it would be possible to measure some specific aspects of ego defenses or adequacy in dealing with the real world, the need for self-preservation is so broad and includes so much territory that it is difficult to know how to start measuring it. It might include not only all aspects of behavior related to achievement and independence, but also dependency, physical comfort needs, and so on. A given response and its opposite might both be taken as evidence of a strong ego. For example, one could explain rationalization, in some circumstances, as necessary for self-preservation and its opposite, self-blame, as an indicator of good reality contact.

While these problems result in certain limitations on what can be accomplished by personality measures, they do not exclude the possibility that such measures can be developed and be useful, at least for limited purposes. When careful test construction, clear theoretical reasoning, and the knowledge of limitations is combined, it is possible to construct useful measures of personality. The methods that psychologists use to assess personality will be described briefly under the following headings: the interview, the questionnaire, projective techniques, observational methods, behavioral techniques, and sociometrics. The methods will be described generally, with only a brief illustration of specific instruments provided.[1]

---

[1] Many readers of this book will be asked at some time to take a personality test for research or other purposes. For this reason, the tests will be described in minimum detail so that the reader can still serve as an unbiased subject.

TECHNIQUES OF PERSONALITY ASSESSMENT

The Interview

The interview is often an expensive way of arriving at a judgment regarding a person's position on some personality variable. It is administered individually, frequently takes a relatively long time, and requires an even longer time to score. Nevertheless, it has many advantages. In order to score an interview, it is often necessary to have a typescript or a recording of the interview session and to have more than one person make a judgment regarding the person's position on the variable(s). That is, it is necessary to have a judge make a rating based on an elaborate set of instructions or a carefully worked out manual. Because these judges must be trained and their reliability in making judgments assessed, the method clearly requires a great deal of examiners' or judges' time. On the other hand, attempts to obtain information in an interview have the advantage of being more personal and more relaxed, the examiner has more opportunity to observe the subject and to make a judgment as to his honesty, his accuracy, and his willingness to cooperate. Thus the interview method often provides very useful information that cannot be obtained by other means. For example, suppose we wish to assess how important it is to an individual to succeed in intellectual endeavors. That is, we want to measure his academic achievement need. If we ask him a series of specific questions, he might deny on all of these that such achievement is very important to him, but in an interview he might spontaneously mention that his father would be extremely pleased if he did well academically and that it is important to him to get his father's approval. While such questions could be incorporated into a questionnaire, the subject might not have answered in the same way in the impersonal atmosphere that exists when people are asked to fill out a questionnaire in a large group setting. In addition, while this kind of information is of importance in understanding the need value of academic achievement for this subject, some other kind of information — perhaps rivalry with a sibling — might be important for understanding the achievement need of another individual. All the things of importance to all the people who might take the test could not easily be incorporated into a single questionnaire. It is possible in an interview for the subject to bring out what is important *to him*.

The techniques of interviewing can be broken down into three broad methods. The first of these is *free* interviewing. In this technique, the interviewer says as little as possible, simply asking open-ended or lead-ing questions. If he were trying to assess the degree of conformity of the subject, he might ask an opening question such as, "Could you tell me something about what the other students in your dormitory are like?" Later on he might add questions such as, "How do you get along with the others in the dormitory?", "What are your friends like?", "What kinds of things do you feel are important to you?", "What do you do in your spare time?" Once the subject has started talking, the interviewer keeps him going by nodding, saying, "Umm-humm, could you tell me more about that?" and so on.

This technique is usually less threatening or disturbing and more re-laxed than when specific and direct questions are asked. It allows the interviewer to see what is important to the subject and to have him ex-pand on these subjects. Because such interviews frequently meander, they often take longer than more direct techniques to obtain all the infor-mation which the interviewer feels he needs in order to make an adequate judgment.

In the second type of interview, the *directed* interview, the interviewer knows which information he wishes to cover and asks many more direct questions. Instead of asking, "Could you tell me what the other students in your dormitory are like?" he asks specific questions about the cloth-ing preferences, attitudes, interests, and customs of the others in the dormitory and then about the student's own clothing preferences, atti-tudes, and interests. He may ask directly, "Do you like to feel different or are you uncomfortable when you differ from the others?" While this method produces more relevant information in a shorter period of time and is easier to score, it has some disadvantages. The subject quickly discovers what is being measured and may decide not to reveal more than he has to. It also falls into a question and answer set, with the sub-ject volunteering very little information except that which is pertinent to the specific question.

In the third method of interviewing, the technique is even more spe-cific. This is usually referred to as the *structured* interview. Here, the interviewer sets up a standard condition for all interviewees. He is re-quired to ask the same questions, generally in the same order, and to use a standard procedure for follow-up questions. While such a method ap-proximates a paper-and-pencil questionnaire, it still has the advantage that the subject's responses are in his own words and can be qualified rather than simply saying, "Yes," "No," or "?" to a questionnaire item. For research purposes, it is somewhat better in that the situation is more

controlled and individual differences in response may be less determined by the personality of the interviewer and the atmosphere he creates. In other words, if one wanted to replicate a study in which this
method of assessment was used, it would be easier for the experimenter
to duplicate the original testing conditions. The structured interview can
also be scored more easily and take less time to administer, but even
more of the advantages of the free interview are lost with this interview
format than with the directed interview.

In order to obtain a score or a rating from an interview, it is necessary
to have someone judge the interview and make a rating. A problem arises, however, if the ratings made by one person cannot be or are unlikely
to be duplicated by another. This is particularly the case if the rating is
based upon the judge's own subjective notions concerning what is to be
measured. Suppose, for example, that the judges were measuring a need
for heterosexual love. One judge might decide that such a need was reflected in the number of dates a person had with members of the opposite sex; another judge might decide that such information was of no particular value since some people, very high in this need, might make few
dates because they could not find people who satisfied their need, and
others might have many dates merely in order to conform and fit in with
their social group or to demonstrate competitive achievement. In other
words, the judges might treat the same data in opposite ways. In order to
avoid this, it is necessary to very carefully define the variable that is being measured, using many examples, and it is useful to provide an explicit written manual, which specifies how different kinds of responses
are to be rated. In order to demonstrate that the manual is adequate and
that the variable can be measured reliably, it is necessary to have more
than one judge rate such interview material and to calculate the degree
of agreement between the judges' ratings. When interscorer reliability is
too low, the technique cannot be used for scientific purposes because it
means that results cannot be duplicated by other investigators.

The Questionnaire

The questionnaire played a prominent role in early attempts to measure personality in the United States. In 1931 Symonds wrote a book
describing methods of measuring personality which was largely devoted
to a variety of questionnaires. However, the questionnaire method gradually fell into disuse as it became more and more obvious that the subject's responses reflected his motivations in taking the test rather than a

true picture of his behavior, feelings, and attitudes. As psychologists became more sophisticated, they developed new methods of constructing questionnaires, so that this technique is again gaining popularity. In general, questionnaires have several advantages: (1) They are easily scored and take little of the examiner's time to administer; (2) The scores are objective, and there is no room for the examiner's bias or distortions to enter into the scoring; (3) The tests can generally be given to several individuals at once and can be scored by persons without specialized training. In other words, questionnaires are very economical, and consequently, they are widely used for screening purposes (that is, they are used when it is necessary to choose individuals from a large group who are in some way at the extreme of the group.

In discussing the values and limitations of questionnaires and self-ratings, it will be useful to illustrate the various forms that they take.

True-False Scale: Circle *true* if the statement below is true about you; circle *false* if it is untrue; and circle the *question mark* if you do not know or cannot make up your mind.

True   False   ?   (1) Most people are out for all they can get.
True   False   ?   (2) I have a hard time making decisions.

Agreement Scale: Make a check on the scale after each statement to indicate the degree to which the statement is true of you.

(1) Most people are out to get all that they can
        Strongly agree   Agree   Agree and Disagree equally
                Disagree   Strongly disagree

(2) I have difficulty in making decisions.
        Never   Rarely   Sometimes   Often   Always

Forced-Choice Scale: Please place a check next to one statement in each pair which you consider to be *more* true about you. One statement *must* be checked in each pair.

(1)   a. Most people are out to get all that they can.
       b. Most people lack the courage of their convictions.
(2)   a. I enjoy talking to people with different backgrounds than my own.
       b. I am most at ease when I am around close friends.

Adjective Check List: Place a check mark next to the adjective in each group which most closely applies to you.

(1) Temperamental   Placid   Worried   Sentimental
(2) Artistic   Athletic   Sociable   Studious

Self-Rating: Below is a list of characteristics. Rate yourself on each of the characteristics by using a check mark to show where you believe that you would be as compared to others of your same age.

HONESTY

1	2	3	4	5	6	7	8	9	10
Least Honest				Average Honesty					Most Honest

CONVENTIONALITY

1	2	3	4	5	6	7	8	9	10
Least Conventional				Average Conventionality					Most Conventional

It can be seen that the true-false type questionnaire is the simplest and usually the quickest to administer and score. However, it has serious problems. Not only are there problems associated with the truthfulness of responses or the subject's motivations, but also with the way in which the subject interprets the questions. When the item says, "I often wonder if it is all worth it," should the subject answer *true* to this if he has such thoughts fleetingly three or four times in the year, or should he say the item is *false* as applied to him? If the item states, "I worry about my future," it would be true of most adults. But some people would answer *false* to this because they feel that it would be giving a false impression if they thought an agreeing response might indicate that they spent a lot of time *seriously* worrying about their future. What do the test constructors have in mind when they ask such a question? What does the subject have in mind when he answers it?

The agreement scale makes up for some of these problems of the true-false format. Instead of merely circling the question mark or impulsively circling either true or false with a feeling that neither is correct, the subject is able to indicate a degree of agreement with an item, making his response at least somewhat more comparable to that of another subject who responds in the same way. This format also allows discrimination between people who strongly agree with a statement and those who only mildly agree with it. This is a distinction which may be very important in the measurement of many personality variables, especially those which are designed to tap attitudes.

The forced-choice scale was developed in order to control the tendency on the part of the subject to respond in a way which he feels is socially desirable. Usually, the paired items are equally desirable or undesirable, or at least approximately equal. It is hard to get subjects to say undesirable things about themselves, except in a situation where they may be seeking help. If we ask subjects to respond true or *false* to, "I easily lose my temper," the great majority of subjects would say "False." However, if we ask them to choose between such an item and another which says, "I usually get depressed," then many of them might choose the first alternative since the second does not put them in any more favorable light. The hope of the test constructor is, of course, that if both statements are equally desirable or undesirable the subject will choose the one which is more true of him. Although this is to some extent true, it is not always the case. It is hard to develop pairs of items in which the social desirability is the same for all testing situations; therefore, what seem to be two equally desirable or equally undesirable statements may not be equal in a particular testing situation. Nevertheless, the forced-choice format does have the distinct advantage that it is possible to get subjects, in rating themselves, to endorse negative items which they would not endorse in the true-false format or agreement scale. This very fact does produce a certain resistance to forced-choice formats, and some subjects find them difficult to take and complain about them. It is also possible that neither alternative tends to be true of that particular subject, and although the instructions generally say, "Select the one which is more true of you," subjects are frustrated by the item and find it extremely difficult to respond.

Adjective check lists of the forced-choice variety have similar advantages and disadvantages to the forced-choice questionnaire. However, they are appropriate only for certain kinds of variables when it is not important to find out how the subject responds to a number of specific things. A subject may be able to describe his current feelings accurately by checking such adjectives as *frustrated, depressed, serene,* and *confident.* But if the examiner wanted to know whether or not the subject was altruistic, it is doubtful that he would know what the subject meant if he checked such an adjective. The subject might mean that he gives money to the community chest regularly, but the examiner may want to know whether or not he goes out of his way to help others, tries hard to give credit to others, and so on. In other words, he has to ask about a number of specific things to get an answer to his question. Broad measures trying to get at temperamental differences, current moods, value systems, areas of adjustment problems, and so on, might be more appropriate for adjective check lists. If we were trying to measure such things as the acceptance of the traditional female role among women, or the orthodoxy of religious belief, or how much honesty is attributed to others, the agreement scale would much more likely be used.

Self-ratings are used only in a few special instances. If we were interested in measuring adjustment or something which we call overall adjustment, we could have a simple self-rating and ask the subject, "How well adjusted are you?" Such an item would at least have the advantage of giving us a statement of degree, in comparison to the simple true-false measure. However, when so much depends upon not only the subject's self-appraisal but also his perception of others, the value of such a simple statement for such a broad variable is questionable. In addition, the subject might be willing to admit to a number of specific problems without being willing to admit that overall he is seriously maladjusted. Consequently, a simple self-rating tends to have very limited value. Nevertheless, self-ratings are sometimes used as very gross measures when little importance is being placed on the accuracy of any single subject's response and when a quick and easy method is sought for measuring group differences. The self-rating can also take the form of a series of items; such a set of items would resemble an agreement scale.

Special techniques are now used to improve the accuracy and value of questionnaire methods. Since it appears that some subjects have a tendency to agree with most items, more sophisticated questionnaires often have items stated in such a way that by agreeing with them all, the subject's score would be in the middle of the distribution. That is, half of the items are written so that agreement puts them at one end of the scale and half so that agreement puts them at the other end of the scale. Other techniques include the use of more subtle items which do not ask questions directly, making it more difficult for the subject to determine exactly what is being measured. Items which have nothing to do with the variable being measured and which are not scored are also sometimes included; these are referred to as *filler* items. Some scales include items which are repeated but stated in a sufficiently different manner so that subjects who are going through the questionnaire carelessly can be identified in that they contradict themselves a number of times. Other scales include items designed to determine whether the subject is making a serious attempt to tell the truth or not. Finally, there are questionnaire scales which make no assumptions about the truthfulness of the responses but essentially treat the responses as an indication of the subjects' general stylistic way of responding, which is presumed to be related to the personality variable being studied; for example, whether they like to agree with extreme statements or whether they never do. In other words, questionnaire tests have become more sophisticated and more subtle so that, to some degree at least, it is more difficult for a subject to deliberately create the particular kind of impression that he feels would be advantageous to him in that situation.

This discussion of questionnaires should not be concluded with an emphasis on their lack of validity because of the conscious distortion of subjects. Many subjects are as honest as they can be, and these tests can be quite useful, especially when one is primarily interested in the average scores of groups of subjects rather than in making predictions about a particular individual. Although their validity is limited for individual prediction, they are often reliable and objective and much useful research is based upon them. An illustration of one such investigation follows.

Katz and Rotter (1969) were interested in investigating the influence of parents on the degree to which college students trusted others. To do this, they used a scale for measuring interpersonal trust developed by Rotter (1967) which used an agreement scale format. The scale included twenty-five items measuring interpersonal trust and some filler items. An example of the kind of item used (but not an actual test item) is, "There are many people who are honest only when it is to their advantage to be honest." The subject would indicate whether he strongly agreed, mildly agreed, agreed and disagreed equally, mildly disagreed, or strongly disagreed.

Katz and Rotter selected 100 male and 100 female college students in residence who had taken the trust scale a year earlier and who were higher or lower than the average student on interpersonal trust. The experimenter sent trust scales directly to the students' parents, asking them to fill them out and return them before the weekend (when their children might come home). Fathers and mothers were asked to answer them independently. Sixty-seven percent complied, which represents a very high return rate for such studies. The parents' scores on their tests are presented in Table 1.

The mean score column of Table 1 shows that the parents of the higher-trusting students were themselves higher in trust than the parents of the low-trusting students, although some some of the differences were small. The largest and most significant effect was that of fathers and sons, contrary to the prediction that would have been made by many psychoanalytic psychologists who would have anticipated a more important role for mothers.

TABLE 1   TRUST SCORES OF PARENTS OF COLLEGE STUDENTS

A. Fathers' Trust Scores

Group	N	Mean	SD
Male Hi Trust	27	79.6	6.21
Male Lo Trust	29	69.4	15.52
Female Hi Trust	28	73.8	13.11
Female Lo Trust	35	72.2	9.63

B. Mothers' Trust Scores

Group	N	Mean	SD
Male Hi Trust	30	77.6	10.16
Male Lo Trust	32	73.8	12.81
Female Hi Trust	33	76.7	14.45
Female Lo Trust	38	73.9	13.06

Fathers and mothers appear to play different roles in the development of trust of others in their children. Fathers seem to play a highly influential role vis-a-vis their sons, but seem to have little effect on their daughters. Mothers, on the other hand, appear to have a small and equal effect on both sons and daughters.

The highly important role that fathers play in influencing their sons' attitudes toward interpersonal trust is not surprising. The variable measured by this scale refers to expectancies for trust of groups of social agents with whom the individual comes into contact outside the family setting. Since the father is usually the major liaison agent between the family and external groups, and is typically more involved in the training of sons than daughters, we would expect that his influence on his son would be maximal.

This study suggests the importance of direct teaching and the importance of parents as models in the development of basic attitudes of children, and it illustrates how a questionnaire can be used to test a theoretical hypothesis regarding the influence of parents on the trusting attitudes of their children.

The list of personality variables which have been measured by questionnaire methods would be very long indeed. Examples of some of these are: anxiety, aggression, adjustment, dependency, need for affiliation, need for achievement, creativity, religiosity, paranoia, independence, need for change, conservatism, liberalism, masculinity, femininity, need for social approval, self-acceptance, interpersonal trust, defensiveness, dominance, submissiveness, and inferiority feelings.

Projective Techniques

Partly to avoid the limitations of self-reports and partly to get at unconscious motivations rather than surface traits and attitudes, a different kind of instrument has received wide use in clinical assessment and personality research. This instrument is generally called a projective technique or test; it differs from other tests in that its administration is informal and the scoring and interpretation is more subjective. Usually a subject is asked to do some simple but imaginative task—to make some drawings, to complete some incompleted sentences, to tell stories about pictures, or to tell what kinds of associations are evoked by particular kinds of stimuli. It is assumed in projective techniques that what a subject produces, whether imaginative or organizational, reveals important and stable characteristics of his own personality.

There are many different kinds of projective techniques; most of them have all or some of the characteristics listed below.

(1) The method is indirect. Compared with the questionnaires, it is more difficult for a subject who wishes consciously to distort to know what represents a "good" versus a "bad" answer or a "right" versus a "wrong" answer. Even when he is unconsciously defensive he is not able to avoid revealing particular aspects of himself because he has no knowledge of what the examiner is seeking. Although this is not completely true of all projective techniques, it is more true of them than of questionnaires. In some instances, particularly in the case of the Rorschach Inkblot Test, the disguise of purpose has been lost for many subjects because of frequent descriptions in newspapers, popular magazines, movies, and television.

(2) There is freedom of response. Freedom of response is the second important characteristic of some of the projective methods. Instead of merely being able to answer yes, no, or question mark, or to indicate the degree of agreement, it is possible to make a great variety of responses to the test stimulus. If asked to tell a story about a picture, a hundred subjects can give a hundred different stories. In this way it is assumed that

the responses of the subject reveal what is important and crucial for him. While one subject, asked to tell stories about a series of pictures, may tell stories mainly concerned with death or suicide, another given the same pictures may tell stories concerned with achievement and success.

(3) Test interpretation deals with many variables. Since it is possible for the subject to respond in many different ways, it is also possible that in interpreting the tests, many different kinds of variables can be assessed or measured. Not all subjects can be measured on the same variables, and this limits some of these instruments for research purposes if the usual method of interpretation is applied. Although it may be possible with one subject to determine how hostile he is, and for another to what extent he is dependent on his mother for emotional satisfactions, the more variables an instrument can potentially measure, the more difficult it is to obtain norms or objective ways of scoring the tests.

Many projective techniques can be scored objectively, but in so doing one loses some of the advantages. In other cases, although the scores may be objective, the interpretation of the scores still requires a great deal of subjective judgment. Also, extensive training and experience is required of test administrators before these instruments can be used wisely. Frequently, the tests require much more time to give, score, and interpret than do other types of personality measures. On the other hand, the trained, experienced examiner has an opportunity to observe a variety of patients in a relatively standard situation and to make judgments about how motives and less obviously important characteristics of each individual determine his behavior.

There is evidence that many situational factors influence responses to projective tests. These too must be assessed by the experienced psychologist. The assumption of disguise of purpose is also not always justified, as has been shown by research findings that subjects can make a better impression if they are instructed to do so. Although in many cases a subject cannot give a good impression, partly because he does not know how to, it is still clear that he will at least react in an inhibited manner if he thinks the test results can be used to put him in a bad light. His test responses will be significantly different from those he gives when he feels that the test is not being used for purposes of selection.

An example of how subjects will change their way of responding in different situations is provided in a study by Henry and Rotter (1956). In this study two groups of thirty female college students were given the Rorschach Inkblot Test. One group, the control group, received the regular instructions, which state that people see different things in the inkblots and that they are to tell the examiner what they see or what the inkblots remind them of and that there are no right or wrong answers. The experimental group got the same instructions, but prior to that they were told—or reminded—that the test had been used in mental hospitals for many years to study emotional disturbances and that it was being used in this experiment to make a college survey. This slight and apparently innocuous addition to the regular instructions, reminding most subjects of what most of them already knew through newspaper articles, television programs, and movies produced marked changes in the mean scores of the two groups. The average total number of responses for each subject in the experimental group was 16 as compared to 23 in the control group. This was a highly significant difference. It meant that the subjects in the experimental group were much more careful in picking out things in the blots in which the form was very clear-cut. That is, they allowed themselves less freedom and imagination. The percentage of popular, or stereotyped, responses rose from 4 percent in the control group to 12 percent in the experimental group.

Not only can slight variations in instructions affect the projective test responses of subjects, but the characteristics of the examiner may also be significant. In fact, such examiner effects can be demonstrated to be significant not only for projective tests but for questionnaires and tests of ability. An example of such a study is an investigation by Mussen and Scodel (1955). They presented two groups of male students with a series of eight slides of attractive nude women and asked the students to rate the attractiveness of each one. Following this they were asked by another experimenter to write stories (for a separate study) for a series of pictures from the Thematic Apperception Test (TAT). The difference between the two groups was that in one group the nude pictures were presented by a formal, professorial, and somewhat stern man in his sixties and in the other group the nude slides were presented by an informal, young-looking, permissive graduate student. As expected, they found that the sexual content in the stories written to the TAT pictures was greater for the group shown the nude pictures by the informal graduate assistant.

In spite of these limitations, however, projective techniques can be quite valuable in providing information not easily obtained by direct methods. A good psychologist regards the judgments he makes from such tests as hypotheses to be dealt with cautiously and, if possible, checked with other kinds of data.

For purposes of additional clarification and illustration, several examples of projective techniques are described below.

Word-Association Test.   A forerunner of the modern projective test still used in clinical settings and in some kinds of personality research is the word-association test. Subjects are given a stimulus word and asked to tell as quickly as possible the first word that comes to mind as an association. The psychologist studies indications of mental or emotional upset revealed by long-delayed responses or other response characterisics as well as the content of the responses. The underlying basis of this test lies in the notion that thought disturbances typical of certain abnormal groups are revealed by the process of association. To this notion Jung, an early colleague of Freud's, added the idea that the association process could reveal unconscious, repressed ideas and serve as a method of discovering "unconscious complexes."

For illustrative purposes, presented below are ten responses given by a hospitalized adult male diagnosed as "schizophrenic" compared to ten common responses of "normal" adults of about the same educational level. The stimulus words are part of the Kent-Rosanoff Word-Association Test.

WORD ASSOCIATION

Stimulus Word	"Normal" Responses	"Schizophrenic" Patient Responses
table	chair	chair
hand	hold	sin
smooth	rough	touch
woman	man	bad
sleep	pillow	death
stomach	eat	open
yellow	blue	fire
bed	sleep	shame
baby	girl	fire
afraid	dark	God

Rorschach Test.   The Rorschach Test is one of the most widely used and most well-known projective techniques. In this test, the subject is presented with a series of inkblots and is asked to tell what they suggest to him. There are no correct or incorrect responses, but what the subject sees in the inkblots presumably reflects his own personality. Originally, the associations were scored and interpreted in such a way that the examiner could compare a subject's responses to those of patients in different categories. The theoretical basis for scoring was that pathological types presumably tended to imagine objects in characteristically different ways. For example, images might be typically visual or kinesthetic. Faculty concepts also play an important role in Rorschach scoring, with different responses representing emotions, will, and intellect. In its current usage, other kinds of variables are assessed from the responses, including those important for the psychoanalytic study of the individual.

Thematic Apperception Test.   In an attempt to measure the needs that are significant variables in his theory of personality, Murray (1943) and his co-workers developed a series of tests of the projective type. Murray assumed that the subject was not usually aware of his own needs and that some instrument to reveal his unconscious thoughts would provide a better understanding than tests that depended on self-report. He felt that fantasy provided such a means of obtaining unconscious motives and devised a series of techniques in which the patient told his fantasies when he was listening to music, or completing incomplete stories, or telling stories about pictures. The latter instrument, in which the subject was asked to tell a story about a picture, became the most widely used of these techniques. There is now available a standard series of pictures for clinical purposes and also special sets of pictures to measure particular variables for both clinical and experimental purposes.

Shown in Figure 2 are pictures of the type used in such tests, although these are not part of any standard series; the verbatim stories told by two different young women follow. They illustrate how different these stories may be. The reader may speculate for himself about the personalities of the two subjects.

PICTURE A

Subject 1. Well, I would say that this girl is about fourteen years old. She has always been shy and stuck pretty close to her mother. One day, when she was walking home from school, a boy asked her to meet him later and go for a walk. She did not know what to say so she just didn't answer him and practically ran all the way home. When she got home, she asked her mother what she should have done, and her mother tried to explain to her about growing up and about boys. She seems quite disturbed about what she is

FIGURE 2 EXAMPLES OF PICTURES USED IN THE THEMATIC APPER-
CEPTION TEST

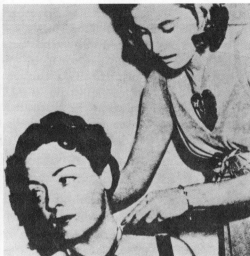

PICTURE A   PICTURE B

Julian B. Rotter, *Clinical Psychology,* © 1964, pages 67–69. Reprinted by
permission of Prentice-Hall, Inc., Englewood Cliffs, New Jersey.

hearing because she really did not want to grow up but wanted to
stay a little girl all her life.

In the end she finally went out with men and married someone
whom her mother suggested.

Subject 2. This is an old picture and an old problem. This girl has
watched her mother gradually drink more and more, and she finally understood what it was to be an alcoholic and why her
mother sometimes stumbled and fell down and would fall asleep
in the living room. She finally accused her mother of drinking,
and the mother is explaining in the picture that she can't help
drinking. The girl asks her mother to stop because she is ashamed
in front of her friends and she thinks the other kids talk about her
mother behind her back, but the mother doesn't stop. Finally, the
mother is taken away to an institution, and when the girl grows

up she leaves town and goes to another place where she is not known.

PICTURE B

Subject 1. These two girls are sisters and they are at a Valentine party. It is a dance and they are getting ready to go down and dance with the boys. Both of them are a little sad and they are thinking that they will not enjoy the dance. The younger sister is helping the older one. The older one is already engaged but at the dance the younger sister finds a boy that she likes very much. She is a little shy at first, but gradually she gets over her shyness, becomes engaged, and marries the boy, and they have five children.

Subject 2. This picture bothers me. I can't tell what the one girl is doing to the other. Let's say that it is two sisters and they are going out on a double date. The one sitting down is the pretty sister and the one standing up is the ugly duckling who has to wait on her pretty sister. She is fixing the pendant around her sister's neck and thinking, "I would really like to choke her." The pretty sister gets all the dates and is the popular one, and the ugly sister only goes out when her pretty sister arranges a double date. The pretty one marries a wealthy man in town and goes to live in a big, beautiful house. But one day she trips going down the stairs and breaks her neck. Once the pretty sister has left the home, people begin to recognize that the ugly sister is not so ugly, and she makes friends on her own and marries a poor boy who really loves her. Her husband goes to work for someone else and for several years they have a hard struggle. Finally, the husband is able to start his own business and he does well, and they become highly respected in the community.

Sentence Completion Method

In the sentence completion method, the subject is asked to finish a sentence, the first word or words of which are given by the examiner. In some ways this method is related to the word-association technique, the major difference being in the length of the stimulus. Some applications of the method, however, demand only a single word or brief response. Many different types of stems are used, and sentence completion tests have been devised to measure a variety of variables. Some examples of different kinds of stems are given below:

I like . . . .   I get angry when . . . .
He worried whenever . . . .   Girls are . . . .

As in the word-association method, tendencies to block or to twist the meaning of the stimulus word may appear, and responses are categorized in a somewhat similar fashion. Even in tests where quickness of response is encouraged, there is no attempt to measure speed of reaction, and no real pressure for *immediate* association. The response tends to provide information that the subject is willing to give, rather than information that he cannot help giving, and analysis is usually more similar to that used with the Thematic Apperception Test than to the word-association method. As in other projective devices, it is assumed that the subject reflects his own wishes, desires, fears, and attitudes in the sentences he composes, but this method differs in that the subject's production does not depend so much upon his interpretation of the standard stimulus as upon what he is able and willing to write under the test conditions.

Observational Methods

Three methods of assessing personality have been described. Two of these, the interview and the standardized questionnaire, are partly limited in that they depend on self-report. The third, the projective technique, does not have the above limitation. However, the responses to projective techniques are influenced by a large number of factors that are not easily identified, the tests themselves require a long time for analysis, and they are potentially subject to the biases of the examiner. All three methods obtain information about subjects in what might be called an artifical or somewhat unnatural situation. Some of the problems inherent in these approaches can be avoided to some extent by the use of behavioral observation techniques.

In these methods the psychologist simply attempts to observe an individual in his natural settings. With children this is sometimes done at home or on the playground. With institutionalized adults it can be done in the ward or, for instance, during occupational therapy.

Scales for rating the behavior of children have been carefully worked out, as have several scales for rating the behavior of hospitalized mental patients. As with projective techniques, it is usually necessary to establish the interrater reliability of the rating scales in order to draw conclusions from such studies. Where the rating is made in a natural setting, it is generally not possible for the observer to hide. In the laboratory he may hide behind a one-way-vision mirror or screen, but in the naturalistic observation situations he must usually be visibly present. To what extent his presence affects the data he is obtaining is not easily determined. It is generally assumed that such an effect occurs, but since it is not possible to obtain the same data with no one present, it is extremely difficult to determine what the effect of the examiner's presence is. From the report of subjects and observers it does appear, at least to some extent, that they get used to the presence of observers and behave naturally even when they know that they are being observed. Nevertheless, despite its advantages of direct observation and naturalness, this method still has its limitations in that the presence of the rater affects the behavior of the person whom he is rating.

One recent way of eliminating the rater is to use a TV camera and later to make ratings from the TV tapes. Whether or not the presence of the camera, the tape of which the subject knows will be studied later, is substantially different from a visible observer still has not been sufficiently studied.

Of course, where a single individual is involved, this method also is quite uneconomical of the examiner's time. For research purposes, however, where a number of individuals are being studied concurrently, the method can be economical. For example, a rater might rate all of the children in a preschool class on specified variables such as constructive play, initiating social contacts, and dependence on teachers. Or an observer could rate all the children in a cottage for delinquents on such variables as fighting, bullying, submissiveness, and so on.

Behavioral Tests

Like the observational techniques just discussed, behavioral techniques tend to rely less on the subject's self-report. However, the behavioral test differs from natural observation in that all the subjects are placed in the same standard test situation. Although the behavioral test loses the advantage of the natural situation by requiring a standard situation, it does avoid one of the limitations of the observational technique. In the natural observation situation one needs to be quite concerned with the adequacy (or representativeness) of the sample of observations. That is, is the time the subject is being observed typical of the usual conditions of that situation? If, for example, a patient in a five- or ten- or fifteen-minute observational period never loses his temper, can it be assumed that he is of placid temperament or merely that nothing happened to frustrate him during that short interval? Since the behavioral test provides everyone with the same situation, there is a sounder basis for comparison.

Of course, all tests measure behavior. The term *behavioral test* is used here to describe those instruments in which the behavior being observed in the standard test situation is the same as or similar to the behavior that the psychologist is interested in predicting in the real-life situation. Instead of asking a person whether he seeks help (is dependent) when he is frustrated or blocked, instead of making an interpretation of dependency from a story he may tell, in the behavioral test the experimenter *does* block or frustrate the subject and then determines on the general basis of fairly objective criteria whether he seeks help or to what extent he seeks help.

In behavioral tests, individuals may be given dull tasks to do to see how long they will persist at them in order to please the examiner. Or they might be put into a group situation where it is necessary for them to cooperate with others in order to solve a number of difficult tasks. Some "frustration" techniques provide insoluble tasks and then make observations of the individual's behavior as he persistently fails in his efforts. For example, one subject may give up easily and say that the task is impossible, another will blame himself but point out that he could solve it if it weren't for the fact that he was up late the night before, and that he hasn't been well lately in any case. A third subject may become angry at the examiner and say the test is stupid and that these psychological experiments are crazy and don't prove anything. Of course, in such testing, it is hoped that such tendencies as that of the first subject to give up easily, and that of the third subject to become aggressive are characteristic of how these persons react to frustration in other situations.

Some of these techniques are called *unobtrusive* tests when the subject is not aware that his behavior is being observed. For example, an observer sitting in the back of a classroom could record the amount of squirming (as a measure of boredom) that went on during a regular class period, making individual comparisons, comparing the whole group under different conditions, or determining how different individuals' squirming behavior changed for different lecturers or different topics.

Sociometrics

Another method which can be of considerable value in the study of personality is sociometric measurement. It combines some of the principles of rating methods and of behavioral observation. In this case, the observer is not an experimenter but a member of some group to which the subject belongs. The method is used where there are groups of people available who know each other reasonably well. Such groups could be found in a classroom, club, fraternity, athletic team, and so on. The members of the group are asked to nominate those people who are high on some characteristic and those who are low, selecting either just one name or a relatively small number of names in comparison to the size of the group. In this way, they have to pick out the people who are, for example, the most friendly, or the most popular, or the least helpful, or the most truthful, or the most worried about their grades. When the names selected by the whole group are put together, it is possible to give a score to each person along a dimension of high to low in the characteristic being measured.

The method has several strengths, the most important of which is that the scores are based upon many observers who can observe the individual in natural settings over a long period of time. It also has the advantage that it is possible to collect data on several variables from the same group of subjects with the same method. The scores obtained in this way are readily comparable. There are two weaknesses to the method, or limitations as to where it can be used. One weakness is that it is necessary to find a suitable group, all of whom know each other quite well. Often this is assumed to be true in the classroom when it is not, in fact, the case. Second, it is necessary to word the instructions for the rating in such a way as to guard against "halo" effect. With some subjects it is almost impossible to do this. *Halo effect* is a technical term for bias on the part of the observers who tend not to discriminate among different characteristics but will rate a particular individual high on all positive traits and low on all negative traits because they like him personally, and vice versa, if they dislike him. Because of this, sociometrics obtained with younger children — that is, grade school age children — are often unreliable. But even with younger children, some kinds of variables, such as popularity, friendship, personal liking, and so on, can be better measured in this way than in any other.

10

Some Empirical Approaches to Personality Study

While the study of personality is often associated with general or global theories, there are many investigators in the field of personality who are interested only in more limited areas of research. Sometimes these investigators develop so-called miniature theories regarding some single variable or a few variables, and sometimes they are only interested in collecting as much empirical data about a single variable or a few related variables as they can. Thus, there are psychologists who work mainly in the field of need for achievement or who are concerned primarily with understanding and predicting aggressive behavior, or whose interest is in the development of independence in children. There are many specific areas of investigation which cannot be covered in this book, but for purposes of illustration four important areas will be briefly presented, with examples of the kind of research that has been done in each area. These four topics are: anxiety, aggression, interpersonal trust, and internal versus external control of reinforcement.

In presenting these studies, our purpose is to illustrate the range and types of studies done in each area. There will be no attempt to cover the areas comprehensively or to arrive at definitive generalizations for each topic. Some of the studies reported clearly grew out of general theories, while others were more empirically oriented.

It will be recalled that the study of personality deals with two kinds of problems. One is concerned with the nature of stable individual differences and the interrelationships of individual-difference variables. The other deals with the processes by which individuals acquire, maintain, and change their characteristics.

Process studies are generally concerned with the effect of various experiences upon some behavior or characteristic. These studies may be longitudinal in nature, being concerned with the effect of early experiences on later behavior, or cross-sectional studies in which the experimenter varies conditions or situations for different groups of subjects and tests immediately afterwards for differences in behavior.

The studies to be reported in this chapter will describe both types of investigations. Some investigations are concerned only with process variables—for example, Berkowitz' (1962) study dealing with the kinds of experiences which produce aggression toward others. Some research, such as the Boroto (1970) investigation on the reliability or unreliability of people who do not trust others, deals only with individual differences. Finally, there are studies which are concerned both with individual differences and with the conditions or processes which govern behavior—for example, Moss' (1961) study of the effects of evaluation stress on cautious behavior. The latter type of investigation in which different experimental (situational) conditions are examined in relationship to individual-difference variables is called an interaction study. This type of investigation often provides useful information that cannot be obtained from the two other types of research.

ANXIETY

Anxiety has long been an important topic of study for psychologists because of the central position of this construct in Freudian psychology. Later it took on additional importance because of the stimulus-response learning theorists who gave it special significance as a motivating force in much social behavior. Dollard and Miller (1950), Mowrer (1950), Brown and Farber (1951), and Spence and Taylor (1953) perceived anxiety as a drive state which motivated the organism to further behavior. Like other drives, such as hunger and thirst, it was an unpleasant state and the organism was motivated to reduce or eliminate it. For Freud and these learning theorists the reduction of anxiety was the basic motive underlying many normal behaviors and most psychopathological behaviors.

One problem with the concept of anxiety is that it has been treated in so many different ways by different writers. For some, it is perceived as a state of fear; others consider fear an unlearned drive and anxiety a learned or secondary drive. Freud distinguished between normal anxiety and neurotic anxiety. The former results from external threats which are real, the latter results from internal threats, that is, from threats of unacceptable unconscious impulses and ideas.

The concept is also complicated in that it has been defined in physiological terms as arousal of the autonomic nervous system, and in psychological terms as an unpleasant feeling of apprehension. When conceived of as a physiological drive state, typical measures of anxiety include such things as sweating palms and a decrease in electrical skin resistance, changes in heart rate, and so on. The term is also used to describe both what might be called a state of the organism, and a personality characteristic. As a state of the organism, anxiety is considered as a temporary condition resulting from some strong stimulation. As a personality characteristic, it presumes to describe either a general level of anxiety different among individuals or a difference in the potential to respond with anxiety, which differs characteristically from one individual to another.

Spielberger (1966) has attempted to clarify this confusion by making a clear-cut differentiation between a state of anxiety and trait anxiety. He defines the state of anxiety as characterized by subjective, consciously perceived feelings of apprehension and tension, accompanied by or associated with activation or arousal of the autonomic nervous system. Anxiety as a personality trait would be defined as an acquired behavioral disposition which predisposes an individual to perceive a wide range of objectively nondangerous circumstances as threatening and to respond to these with anxiety-state reactions disproportionate in intensity to the magnitude of the objective danger. According to Spielberger then, anxious people are characterized by the fact that they perceive danger or threat to a greater extent than do others or in situations in which others see no objective danger or threat at all.

What are the effects of high anxiety upon performance? Mandler and Sarason (1952) have hypothesized that when an anxious subject is faced with a stressful task, he makes responses which are irrelevant to task completion (e.g., thinking about the consequences of failure), and these responses can interfere with successful task performance. Mandler and Watson (1966) did the following experiment to test this hypothesis. They told subjects that they had two tests for them to take; one was described as a standard intelligence test known to be a good predictor of intellectual capability, and the other was described as a test about which they were collecting data in order to see whether or not it would be a useful and valid measure. Each test was to be given five times so that enough data could be collected to make a "meaningful" comparison of the two tests.

They divided their subjects into two groups. One group was allowed to choose before each trial the order in which they preferred to take the tests. The other group was told they had to take the tests in a prearranged order for administrative reasons. Mandler and Watson had previously given the subjects a test-anxiety questionnaire which provided a score for a characteristic tendency to become anxious in test-taking situations. Before the experiment, they selected subjects who were high-anxious and low-anxious according to this questionnaire, and consequently they had four groups of subjects: high-anxious subjects who could exercise control over the order of the tests they took, and high-anxious subjects who could not exercise such control; low-anxious subjects who could exercise control, and low-anxious subjects who could not exercise control. They hypothesized that the high-anxious subjects would do more poorly than the low-anxious subjects on the "real" test of intelligence. They also hypothesized that not having control over the order of the tests would increase the stressfulness of the situation and that the subjects with no control would do more poorly than subjects with control.

The required task for both tests was a digit-symbol substitution test which entails rapid, concentrated work, and the two tests were actually two forms of a test commonly used as a subtest in some intelligence scales. Additional instructions were employed to make the so-called "real" test of intelligence important and stressful and the exploratory test relatively less important for the subjects.

The results that they obtained for the "real" intelligence test are shown in Figure 3. No significant differences between high-anxious and low-anxious subjects were found for the exploratory or experimental digit substitution test. The figure clearly shows support for their hypotheses; high-anxious subjects did more poorly than low-anxious subjects on the "real" test, and subjects with no control did more poorly than subjects with control. Mandler and Watson also gave their subjects a questionnaire following the experimental procedure, asking them how often during the testing they found themselves thinking how well or how badly they were doing and how often during the testing they found themselves wondering about how well other students might perform. They found for both of these questions that the high-anxious groups reported more of such obsessive or ruminative thoughts than the low-anxious subjects and felt that this supported their theory that anxiety tends to

FIGURE 3   MEAN DIGIT-SYMBOL SUBTEST PERFORMANCE ON THE SIIT
OVER FIVE TRIALS (N = 8 PER GROUP)

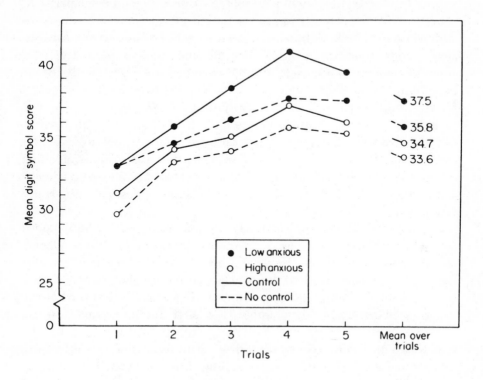

Fig. 2, George Mandler and David L. Watson, in *Anxiety and Behavior,* Charles D.
Spielberger (Ed.). New York: Academic Press, 1966. p. 274.

interfere with task performance because of implicit responses which interfere with successful task completion. While the results of this study
can also be used to support other theories of how anxiety functions, they
do tend to support an interruption or interference theory of the relationship of anxiety to intellectual performance.

Conflict is usually defined as a state of the organism resulting from the
opposition of two or more strong motives or drives. All of us would will-
ingly avoid situations which make us anxious or fearful if it were not for
the fact 'that other motives pull us into such situations. Epstein (1962)
was interested in the effects of experience upon such conflict situations,

and he decided to study the reactions of parachute jumpers as a model for approach-avoidance conflicts. Since parachute jumping is entirely a voluntary activity, one might assume that parachute jumpers experience little fear. This apparently is not the case. But other motives which are stronger direct the individual into such an activity despite his fear. Epstein studied four groups of jumpers: the first group were novices who were on their first to fourth jump; the second group had had only five to eight jumps; a third group had had twenty to thirty jumps; and, finally a fourth group that had made over a hundred jumps. Epstein measured their basal skin conductance before and after a jump. A high level of conductance was interpreted as indicating tension, or anxiety, or general level of activation. A lower level of conductance was seen as reflecting the subjective feeling of euphoria that subjects reported following a jump. There were six subjects in each of the four groups. Results of the study are shown in Figure 4.

It is clear in Figure 4 that anxiety or tension was very high for the novice jumpers, but with increased experience (groups 2 and 3) the general level of tension decreased. However, the last group, those persons who had made over one hundred jumps, showed both higher anxiety before the jump and less euphoria after the jump than did the group who had experienced twenty to thirty jumps. This latter finding was unexpected and Epstein was not sure whether or not in this type of dangerous activity it was typical for anxiety to build up again following a period of extinction or whether there was something different about the kinds of people who persisted in parachute jumping for such a long time.

Often, studies in personality follow common sense, and laymen sometimes wonder why such studies are necessary when everyone knows what the outcome will be. Surely, it could be expected that if people persisted in parachute jumping they would be more frightened at first than they are later. However, we frequently discover things which do not follow common sense, and in this case the reason for the striking rise in basal skin conductance in Epstein's highly experienced group is still not clear and only further research may clarify it.

What is the relationship between anxiety and cautious behavior? A study investigating this question was conducted by Moss (1961). Moss' study utilized social learning theory concepts. Consequently, he did not use the concept of anxiety. In social learning theory the anxiety construct is not used as such because it has too many meanings. Instead the idea of expectancy of failure or expectancy of negative reinforcement is used, and this notion overlaps heavily with at least some conceptions of

FIGURE 4 BASAL CONDUCTANCE BEFORE AND AFTER A JUMP AS A FUNCTION OF EXPERIENCE

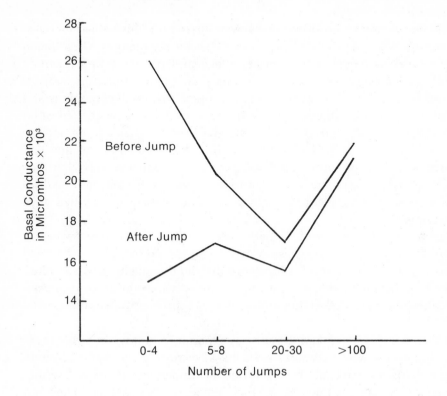

Reprinted from "The Measurement of Drive and Conflict in Humans: Theory and Experiment" by Seymour Epstein, in the Nebraska Symposium on Motivation, by permission of University of Nebraska Press and the author. Copyright © 1962 by the University of Nebraska Press.

anxiety. Moss' experiment involved three steps. In the first phase of the experiment, he gave each subject a level-of-aspiration test (Rotter, 1954). In this test the subject is asked to go through a series of trials involving a motor-skill task, and before each trial he is asked to state as accurately as he can what score he expects to get. Previous research has shown that certain patterns of goal setting which might be called either cautious or noncautious emerge and are characteristic of different individuals. Cautious subjects tend not to overestimate and to expect scores close to their previous performances. The noncautious subjects tend to overestimate more, that is, they expect to do better than they did the last time and are more persistent in setting high goals even after experiencing failures on earlier trials.

In the second phase of his study, Moss gave all of his subjects a questionnaire which he labeled as a test of "social acceptability." Although some subjects might deny it, most college students are quite concerned with their acceptance by others. At this point in the study, the subjects were divided into three groups, each group containing half cautious and half noncautious subjects. The first group of subjects were told, after they had taken the questionnaire and the experimenter had apparently scored it, that they had done very well and had come out at the 90th percentile in social acceptability. The second group was told that they had done poorly and had come out only at the 10th percentile. The third group was given no feedback or information on how well they had done on the test.

In the third phase of the experiment, all the subjects were given two projective type tests, and these were reliably scored by judges who rated the subjects' degree of cautiousness—that is, the extent to which their test responses tended to be "safe," unimaginative, conforming responses. The results were interesting and somewhat surprising. The group who had had the failure experience were, overall, the most cautious, followed by the group who had had the success experience. But the control group, those subjects who had had no feedback, were the least cautious. Success in this study did not lead to lowered cautiousness. Perhaps this finding explains some of the conservatism of people who are established and successful. It was as if, having been told that they did so well on the first questionnaire, the successful subjects decided to be very careful on the two remaining tests so as not to lose their high but perhaps shaky status. When one examines the differences between the cautious and noncautious subjects within groups, it is clear that most of the differences among the groups are the result of differences in the behavior of the noncautious subjects. The cautious subjects tended to be cautious on both tests and in all conditions. However, the noncautious subjects were made more cautious both by an extreme failure and a strong success experience. When they were given no feedback (in the control condition), they continued showing their characteristic noncautious behavior in the third phase of the experiment. It was only in the no-feedback conditions that there was a large and significant difference between the cautious and noncautious subjects.

Mention was made earlier of the greater value of the interaction design for studying personality. This kind of study, which focuses on both individual differences and differences in experimental conditions, illustrates the value of such a design quite clearly. If only individual differences had been studied—that is, if we found whether or not the level-of-aspiration behavior predicted behavior on the projective tests—probably a strong relationship would have been found, since this would be most like the no-feedback condition. However, we would not have known that this kind of consistency would be considerably reduced following either strong success or failure. On the other hand, if Moss had not divided his groups on the basis of the level-of-aspiration tests as a measure of individual differences, we would have concluded that both failure and success produced more cautious behavior than does no feedback. This conclusion would have been true only for the noncautious subjects and not for the subjects who are characteristically cautious. In fact, it was under the no-feedback condition that the cautious subjects were the most cautious in the last phase of the study. For them, not having information about how well they had done on the first test was more disturbing than being told that they had done either very poorly or very well.

How does one reduce stress or anxiety resulting from a threatening stimulus? To study this question Lazarus and Alfert (1964) measured reactions to a "subincision" movie shown to male college students. The film depicts part of a coming-of-age rite in a primitive tribe, showing a painful and bloody operation performed on the penises of young boys. Lazarus and Alfert were interested in the effects of cognitive appraisal in reducing the stress of threatening situations. They presented the film to three groups of subjects in three different ways. In the first condition, the seventeen-minute film was shown without introduction or commentary. In the second condition, which they called the denial and reaction-formation condition, a commentary which accompanied the film denied the harmful aspects of the ritual—the commentator underplayed the pain and potential physical harm and stressed the pleasure experienced by the young boys in taking part in this ceremony of manhood. In the third condition, the denial and reaction-formation commentary preceded the showing of the film, rather than accompanying it as was the case in the second condition.

To measure the effects of the stressful film, the experimenter continuously recorded skin conductance changes and heart rate. Following the film, three additional measures involving verbal reports on the part of the subjects were obtained to assess subjects' expressed feelings about the film.

Lazarus and Alfert found that the first condition, with no commentary accompanying or preceding the film, produced the greatest autonomic changes (changes in skin conductance and heart rate). The film with the accompanying commentary denying the negative aspects of the operation produced the next greatest autonomic changes. The least amount of anxiety was aroused by the film with the commentary preceding it. These results supported their hypothesis that cognitive appraisal could change the threatening or stressful value of the stimulus. If one can regard things which are ordinarily frightening in a different light, they become less frightening.

Before the experiment was completed, the subjects took the Minnesota Multiphasic Personality Inventory. This test can be scored for tendencies to deny or repress unpleasant facts about oneself. When subjects were divided into groups of high-deniers and low-deniers on the basis of their scores on this test, it was found that the high-deniers reacted more to the denial commentary when describing their feelings after the showing of the film. That is, their verbal responses indicated that the commentary reduced anxiety to a greater extent for them than it did for the subjects who did not show strong denial tendencies on the Minnesota Multiphasic Personality Inventory. In spite of what they said, the high-deniers tended to show higher levels of autonomic arousal than the low-denial subjects. These findings illustrate the problem discussed in Chapter 8 with regard to verbal questionnaires. When subjects are asked to admit to negative characteristics about themselves, verbal responses are often not correlated with other behavioral measures. In some cases, the subjects who most strongly deny having negative characteristics may be the most disturbed. The distortion of verbal responses, as in the present study, is often not conscious; thus the issue is not merely that the subject is not telling the truth, but that he is not aware of his own feelings.

AGGRESSION, HOSTILITY, AND ANGER

In early conceptions of personality, aggressiveness was usually considered to be an instinct. It was believed that everyone had an instinct to attack others, and that the aggressive instincts of certain people, races, or groups were especially strong. Freud considered such an instinct part of the group of instincts which he called the death instinct. Usually, people who believed in such an instinct felt that wars were inevitable because somehow or other humans had to express their aggressive instincts. Others felt that the problem of peace was one of controlling, curbing, or sublimating the aggressive instinct which was presumed to be present in everyone. In 1939, Dollard, Doob, Miller, Mowrer, and Sears published a book called *Frustration and Aggression*, which was very influential in the experimental study of aggression. While they did not entirely abolish the instinct concept (maintaining the belief that aggression was an inborn response potential), they specified that aggression resulted from frustration. All frustration led to aggression; all aggression was preceded by frustration. The implication was that if there were no frustration, there would be no aggression. But, in fact, since human beings are never entirely free from frustration, this formulation was not too different from the earlier pure-instinct conceptions.

The study of aggression has been plagued to some degree by the same problems as the study of anxiety. Definitions of aggression include an internal state, which is sometimes referred to as anger, and a behavioral definition emphasizing behavior directed toward the injury of others. Some very broad definitions leave room for a great variety of behaviors, including so-called injury to oneself or "aggression turned inward," therefore encompassing such things as "guilt" and "lowered self-esteem." As for the state of anger itself, definitions also vary with regard to their emphasis on subjective feelings versus physiological descriptions.

Current researchers, however, have been mostly interested in aggression defined as behavior directed toward the injury of others. Most studies are concerned with the conditions which lead to such behavior, with individual differences in the potential to respond with such behavior, or with the interaction of situational influences and individual differences.

What are the antecedents of aggressive behavior as a personality characteristic? In order to answer this question, McCord, McCord, and Howard (1961) studied the parental behavior of groups of children who could be characterized as aggressive, assertive, or nonaggressive. To obtain their aggressive children they avoided the use of delinquents, since it is clear that many delinquents are passive followers. There is also some question of whether or not delinquents are really more aggressive than nondelinquents, since many children (especially middle-class, white children) are equally or more aggressive than the average delinquent but do not come to the notice of the police or, when caught, are not placed in institutions. They selected their subjects from a large group of children referred to the Cambridge-Somerville Youth Study of the 1930s.

These children had been visited in their homes, and ratings had been made of parental behavior; in addition, reports on the children were obtained from psychiatrists, physicians, camp counselors, and school personnel.

The experimenters selected twenty-five boys who were considered to be consistently and overtly aggressive. These children were frequently involved in fist fighting, bullying smaller children, attacking their teachers, or acting destructively in camp or in the community. Ninety-seven boys were classified as assertive. These boys, at times, participated in fights, acts of destruction aimed at other children or adults, and occasional battles with teachers or other community officials. They differed from the openly aggressive boys, however, in that their hostile responses were sporadic exceptions to the general pattern of their lives. In school they sometimes created disciplinary problems for the teacher, but usually they conformed to the standards of the school. Fifty-two boys were classified as consistently nonaggressive. For these children, outbursts of rage or aggressive behavior were rare. Their relationships with other children could be characterized as placid and friendly, and they could apparently absorb the usual frustrations of childhood calmly and realistically.

The basic data of the study came from professionals who made ratings from the notes of staff personnel who directly observed the family in the home over a five-year period. The authors of this study felt that they had minimized a possible source of bias in these observations, since the ratings were made over a long period of time and by different people. The home observations were also made long before their study so that the observers were not aware that their observations would be used for a study of aggressive behavior. The professional raters were likewise unaware that the data would be used for a study of aggression, and they were not acquainted with the hypotheses being tested. Some of their findings are listed below:

(1) The aggressive boys and the assertive boys were more likely than the nonaggressive boys to have been disciplined in a punitive fashion by their mothers.

(2) The aggressive boys were more likely than the assertive boys and the nonaggressive boys to have been frequently threatened by their parents.

(3) The aggressive boys were more likely than the assertive or the nonaggressive boys to have been raised by parents who rejected them.

(4) The aggressive and the assertive boys were more likely than the

nonaggressive boys to have been raised by parents who did not impose high demands on them.

(5) The aggressive boys and the assertive boys were less likely than the nonaggressive boys to have been closely supervised by their parents.

(6) The nonaggressive boys and, to a lesser extent, the assertive boys were more likely than the aggressive boys to have been disciplined by their mothers in a consistent fashion.

In addition to the specific information about the effects of certain childrearing practices, the authors felt that, in general, the study strongly suggested that although the capacity for rage is inborn, the development of a trait involving aggressive behavior depends to a large extent on the culture as it is mediated by early familial experiences.

Although this study did not include all of the possible antecedents to consistent aggressive behavior (such as the effects of siblings and friends and personal characteristics which may have made subjects appear different from others), the authors did find a large number of significant differences in parental behavior for the children of these three different groups.

The relationship between feelings of hostility, anger, or aggression and overt aggressive behavior has been a frequent subject of study. It is obvious to everyone, on the basis of personal experience, that people can feel angry but can control any overt expression of their anger. Consequently, the person who expresses the most aggression is not always the one who is most easily instigated to anger. Of course, it is difficult to know whether people feel angry or not if they do not show their anger in overt behavior and perhaps even deny it to themselves. One way of getting at such feelings is through the use of fantasy techniques, such as asking subjects to tell stories about a set of pictures, as is done in the Thematic Apperception Test (TAT) (see Chapter 9). Mussen and Naylor (1954) used this technique to study the relationship between overt and fantasy aggression. Their subjects were twenty-nine lower-class institutionalized boys. These boys all had been placed in a juvenile home for diagnostic study following some act of delinquency. The overt aggressive behavior of these boys was measured through daily behavior reports in which specific aggressive behaviors were checked by observers over a period of time. A second measure involved weekly ratings made by the cottage personnel. Subjects all took the Thematic Apperception Test, and these tests were scored for aggressive themes and also for themes indicating a fear of punishment for aggression. Mussen and Naylor found that there was a direct relationship between the amount of overt aggression and the frequency of aggressive themes in the TAT stories. There was also a significant effect of fear of punishment. Those subjects who showed the highest aggressive themes and the lowest fear of punishment were very high on overt aggression as measured both by weekly ratings and daily observations of aggressive acts. Similarly, those who were both low on aggression themes and high on fear of punishment showed the least overt aggression. It is clear from this study that fear of punishment is an important variable in the prediction of overt aggression. The study also illustrates the utility of projective tests such as the Thematic Apperception Test for measuring consistent personality characteristics.

The investigation by Mosher, Mortimer, and Grebel (1968) attacked the same problem in a somewhat different way. In the Mussen and Naylor study, punishment themes in the TAT were very broadly defined and included injury to a loved object, deprivation of privileges, and expressions of dislike, as well as injury to the hero as a direct consequence of the hero's aggression. In the Mosher, Mortimer, and Grebel study, inhibition of verbal aggression was investigated in relationship to the hostility or aggressiveness of another person.

Their subjects were 128 delinquent boys incarcerated in a state school for delinquents. On the basis of discussions with a social worker and the cottage parents, four groups whose aggressive characteristics were agreed upon were selected. The first of these groups were called the powerful-aggressive boys. They were physically strong, usually dominated the group, were feared by the others, and achieved this position through their overt aggression and bullying of the others. The second group were called powerful-nonaggressive. These boys were respected in the group and not bothered by the bullies, but they did not attempt to control the other boys through threats, fighting, or other aggressive means. The third group were characterized as weak-resistive. These boys tended to be the targets of the more dominant members; they did attempt to fight back and retaliate with threats and insults, but they were attacked frequently and usually lost their battles. The fourth and final group were called weak-submissive boys. They, too, were frequently chosen as targets for aggressive behaviors, but they submitted without fighting back.

These boys were placed in an experimental situation in pairs. Each pair was told that they were competing to see who could complete a complicated task involving form perception most quickly and that they were allowed to distract, anger, or upset the other person by saying anything they wished while the other subject was working. In this situation, the verbal comments of the subjects encouraged to aggress were recorded and scored according to a precise scoring system. The experimenters had used the same technique in an earlier study which demonstrated that the stronger the aggressive attack on the subject while he was working, the more aggressive the victim was in his retaliation when the roles were reversed. After one subject completed the task, the roles were reversed and the other subject then attempted the task while the first one had an opportunity to retaliate with verbal aggression. The results were clearly as predicted. The powerful-aggressive subjects were the most verbally aggressive, followed by the powerful-nonaggressive and the weak-resistive groups, with the weak-submissive subjects showing the least amount of verbally aggressive behavior. In terms of amount of aggressive verbalizations received, the order of the groups was reversed from the above, with the powerful-aggressive subjects receiving the least, and the weak-submissive subjects the most verbal abuse. The fact that the subjects who were most aggressive were aggressed against the least, while the least aggressive subjects were aggressed against the most may be partially a function of this particular experimental design. Each subject was paired with a boy from another group; therefore, the powerful-aggressive boys were in all cases paired with someone less aggressive than they, while the weak-submissive boys were in all cases paired with someone more aggressive than they. We might expect somewhat different results if the same study were done using pairs of equally aggressive and equally non-aggressive subjects. Nevertheless, the results clearly indicate that fear of retaliation is a powerful controller of overt aggression. But the tendency to fear retaliation, like aggressiveness itself, can be regarded as a consistent personality characteristic. It seems from this study that human beings in some situations may well form pecking orders (similar to those established by lower animals) in which there is a hierarchy for the expression of aggression, with those in the middle inhibiting aggression toward the more powerful but expressing it freely toward the less powerful members of a group.

Both the study of Mussen and Naylor and the study of Mosher, Mortimer, and Grebel are largely derived from and provide support for Rotter's social learning theory. In both studies it was hypothesized that an expectancy for punishment as a direct result of aggression mediated between a desire to aggress and overt aggressive behavior. As the expectancy for punishment increased, overt aggressive behavior decreased.

An interesting aspect of the study of personality involves the investigation of sex differences in behavior. A cultural stereotype in our society is that men are more aggressive than women. Berkowitz et al. (1962) set out to investigate this belief using male and female college students as subjects.

In this investigation the subjects were brought into the experimental room in same-sex pairs to work on problems and were told that this was a study of problem solving under stress. The stress was created by having each subject serve as a judge, evaluating the other's performance by giving him one or more shocks. The subjects specified how many shocks should be given, but the experimenter administered the shocks arbitrarily, giving the other member of the pair a prearranged number of shocks. After being shocked, each subject served as an evaluator for the person he believed shocked him. Half of the subjects were angered by giving them the maximum number of shocks (implying the worst performance) and the other half were given only one shock (implying the best performance). What was measured in this experiment was the number of shocks given by the subject to his partner after he had been shocked himself (Trial I). There were, then, two groups of subjects, those who were angered after receiving the maximum number of shocks and those who had received the minimum number and were presumably not angry. These groups were further subdivided into two groups. One half of them were shown a fake "poor" performance for the subject they were evaluating before deciding how many shocks the other person should have and half were shown a fake "good" performance. The maximum number of shocks that could be administered was seven, the minimum, one.

After they decided on how many shocks to administer to their partner, they were asked to fill out some questionnaires while the partner was presumably working on the second problem. Also at this point they were shown a fake "moderately good" performance and asked a second time (Trial II) to administer shocks to the partner.

The results of this study showed clearly that the angered subjects, those who received more shocks, administered more shocks to their partners. Overall, men and women did not differ in the number of shocks administered but both gave more shocks for the poor performance which Berkowitz regarded as providing a social sanction for their hostility. Nevertheless, there are some interesting differences. For one thing, in the angered condition, the women gave a larger number of shocks on Trial II when the partner had done good work on the first trial and significantly fewer shocks in Trial II when the partner had done poor work on the first trial. It is as if the women stayed angry longer when the partner had done good work, but felt guilty after delivering a high number of shocks when the partner had done poor work. Overall, women were not less aggressive than men, but they appeared to make a greater distinction between those who did poorly and those who didn't, and they tended either to be more inhibited or to feel more guilty in aggressing towards someone who was apparently less competent.

Although some sex differences in personality may have a consitutional basis, it is likely that most of them are the result of different kinds of experiences in childhood. In some cultures, sex differences which are characteristic of our society are reversed. In any case, with the rapid changes now going on in our society with regard to sex roles, many characteristic sex differences may also be changing.

INTERPERSONAL TRUST

It is belaboring the obvious to discuss the significance of interpersonal trust in our society. It seems clear that disarmament will not proceed without an increase in trust on one or both sides of the iron curtain. The entire fabric of our day-to-day living—of our social order—rests on trust. Buying gasoline, paying taxes, going to the dentist, flying in an airplane, almost all of our decisions involve trusting someone else. The more complex the society, the greater the necessity for depending upon others.

The research to be described in this section deals with trust of others as a generalized personality characteristic and is primarily concerned with individual differences. The conception of trust derives from social learning theory (see Chapter 8), and this section can be viewed as an example of the application of a general theory to an important practical problem.

Interpersonal trust is defined in social learning theory as an expectancy held by an individual or a group that the word, the promise, or the verbal or written statement of another individual or group can be relied upon. If such expectancies are generalized and constitute a relatively stable personality characteristic, they should be readily amenable to investigation.

In order to investigate trust as a personality variable, it was necessary to develop a measure or test of trust and to determine whether the measure was valid—that is, whether it would be able to predict behavior in a variety of situations.

To begin this process, Rotter (1967a) developed an agreement type scale using such items as, "Most people really mean what they say." Subjects were required to indicate the degree to which they agreed or disagreed with each item. In order to make a first assessment of the validity of this scale, it was given to college students who were members of two sororities and two fraternities. All of the subjects had lived in their groups for at least six months and were well known to each other. The test scores could then be compared to ratings made by a large group of peers who had had considerable opportunity to observe whether or not each subject was trusting or distrusting. A sociometric technique was used, in which each person in the group nominated the three most trusting and the three least trusting members of their group. In addition to being asked to nominate members of the group who were highest and lowest on interpersonal trust, subjects were also asked to nominate people for three other variables which might be related to trust—gullibility, dependency, and trustworthiness. In order to determine whether they were merely ranking as high on trust the people that they liked best, three other variables were included as *control* variables. They were humor, popularity, and friendship. The correlations of the trust scale with the seven variables are shown below in Table 2. The correlations between the test scale and the seven sociometric variables are shown in the first column; the second column shows the correlations between sociometric trust as rated by peers and the other six sociometric measures. The higher correlations in the second column probably are partially the result of a "halo effect"—that is, a tendency to rate people who are high on one positive characteristic as also being high on other positive characteristics, and vice versa for negative characteristics.

The correlations in the first column show that the interpersonal trust scale indeed has some validity in predicting behavior as observed by others. The correlation of .38 between the trust scale and sociometric ratings, although only moderate, is significantly higher than that of the trust scale with any of the other variables except for trustworthiness. One conclusion that can be reached from this study is that the interpersonal trust scale can predict everyday behavior significantly better than chance, implying that there is indeed generality to trust behavior. It also can be seen from the correlations of the trust scale with sociometric trustworthiness that these two variables are closely associated. Another conclusion of interest is that most people view trusting behavior in others as a positive characteristic.

The correlations in the second column show that people who are seen as high in trust are also seen as trustworthy—that is, as likely to tell the truth themselves. They are popular, regarded by many as friends, and, although to a lesser extent, perceived as having a good sense of humor. They are not regarded as being dependent or gullible.

TABLE 2   CORRELATION OF THE INTERPERSONAL TRUST SCALE WITH
SOCIOMETRIC VARIABLES (N = 156)

Sociometric Trust	.38
Sociometric Trustworthiness	.31
Sociometric Dependency	−.23
Sociometric Humor	.09
Sociometric Gullibility	−.03
Sociometric Popularity	.20
Sociometric Friendship	.19

Does personality affect political attitudes and behavior? Hamsher, Geller, and Rotter (1968) had an opportunity to study this question when interest in the Warren Commission Report was revived as a result of the activities of the district attorney in New Orleans. The Warren Commission was appointed by President Johnson to investigate the circumstances of the assassination of President Kennedy. The significance of the Commission was that it was composed of people whom the public would be most likely to trust. While the Warren Commission found no evidence for a conspiracy in the assassination of President Kennedy, various individuals believed that there was, in fact, such a conspiracy. Hamsher, Geller, and Rotter sampled a large number of college students' attitudes toward the Warren Commission Report. Using only those students who felt they had sufficient knowledge of the subject, they compared a group which accepted the Warren Commission's findings as essentially correct and honest with a group of subjects who believed not only that the Warren Commission Report was wrong, but that this committee of men of supposedly unimpeachable reputation knew of a conspiracy and were deliberately covering it up.

Many of these students in these two groups had taken the trust scale in large psychology classes at an earlier time. Although there were no items on the trust scale that dealt with political preferences, the investigators nevertheless found a clear-cut relationship between trust measured as a personality variable and whether one believed or disbelieved the Warren Commission Report. The differences were large and reliable.

An interesting sidelight of this study was that in answer to a specific question asking whether or not the subject believed that there was a conspiracy and that the Warren Commission knew of this but kept the knowledge from the public, 28 percent of the subjects responded positively. Nineteen percent said, "I don't know," and only 52 percent said, "No." These figures are not much different from those of public opinion polls which asked a similar question. The fact that only half of the general public believed the statement made by a group of leaders who were considered to have a reputation for honesty is a disturbing commentary on current society.

The previous study suggests that we are not a highly trusting people. Has this always been the case or has there been a recent drop in trust of others? Hochreich and Rotter (1970) investigated the latter question among college students.

Hochreich and Rotter had access to scores on the Interpersonal Trust Scale which was given every fall semester, under comparable testing conditions, to a large class of elementary psychology students. The data is now available for a study of changes over time for the years 1964 through 1971, a period of eight years. The findings are shown in Table 3. It can be seen that each year the average trust score fell, except for the period 1970–1971 when it appears to have leveled off. The drop from year to year for previous years was statistically significant. It can be seen from Table 3 that the number of students involved was indeed large and the drop was consistent for both males and females. The total drop over the eight-year period was very large. Stated in statistical terms, one could say that a subject who was at the mean of the distribution of scores in 1970 or 1971 would have been in the lower 20 percent in 1964.

Analyses were made of all of the samples to determine whether or not there were other variables which would account for the drop. These analyses indicated that there were no significant changes in class rank, in college entrance examination scores, in ethnic or racial composition, or in test-taking attitudes which could account for the consistent drop in trust scores.

Hochreich and Rotter examined each item in the trust scale, comparing samples collected during 1964 and 1969 to determine whether the drop in trust was general or was restricted to specific areas of trust. This analysis showed that almost all items dropped somewhat over the period, suggesting a generalized drop in trust, but that some items fell considerably more than others. The items that showed the greatest decrease included those in the areas of politics, peace keeping, and communications. The items that showed little or no change included those dealing

TABLE 3 MEANS AND STANDARD DEVIATIONS OF SCORES ON THE INTERPERSONAL TRUST SCALE, 1964–1971

Test administered	Sex	N	M	SD
September 1964	Male	248	•73.01	10.23
	Female	299	71.91	9.95
	Combined	547	72.41	10.90
September 1965	Male	312	71.74	10.78
	Female	450	71.31	9.64
	Combined	762	71.48	10.11
September 1966	Male	248	70.20	9.40
	Female	329	70.50	8.92
	Combined	577	70.30	9.12
September 1967	Male	174	69.16	9.42
	Female	63	69.52	9.57
	Combined	237	69.34	9.46
September 1968	Male	191	67.71	9.05
	Female	132	67.88	11.20
	Combined	323	67.78	9.98
September 1969	Male	522	66.54	9.19
	Female	646	66.73	10.00
	Combined	1168	66.64	9.69
September 1970	Male	233	65.08	6.30
	Female	230	64.35	10.20
	Combined	463	64.72	9.55
September 1971	Male	454	66.07	8.94
	Female	480	64.72	9.96
	Combined	934	65.37	9.60

with social agents with whom the subjects were likely to have had some direct contact, such as parents, repairmen, salesmen, or ordinary people.

In a study whose primary focus was investigation of sex guilt, Boroto (1970) obtained an interesting incidental finding regarding trust and moral behavior. Boroto's subjects were brought into a room where he presumably had some personal information about them in a folder and where he also accidentally knocked over a folder containing "filthy pictures" on his way out of the office to answer a telephone call. Scooping up the pictures and replacing them in the folder, he left the office where the subjects were being observed surreptitiously.

Most of Boroto's subjects had taken the trust scale two months earlier. When Boroto divided his subjects into those who looked into the folder involving their personal information, or the dirty pictures, or both, and compared them with those subjects who did not invade the experimenter's privacy, he found considerable difference in the mean trust scores. Those who looked at neither folder had a mean interpersonal trust score of 80, and those who looked at either of the folders averaged a score of 66. The difference is not only highly statistically significant, but is approximately one and a half standard deviations different. The average score for those who looked at either folder was close to the mean of the larger population. It was those who did not look at either folder who were deviant, in that they were unusually high on trust. Interestingly enough, in a later interview, about half of the subjects who had looked at the folders denied looking at them.

INTERNAL VERSUS EXTERNAL CONTROL OF REINFORCEMENT

The importance of reinforcement or reward in determining future behavior is recognized by almost all psychologists. However, it has become increasingly clear that such effects of reinforcement do not follow from a simple stamping-in process; at least with human beings, the effects depend upon whether or not the person perceives a *causal* relationship between his own behavior and the reward. Rotter (1966, 1972) and his colleagues have presented considerable evidence that people learn differently in situations where rewards depend upon chance, luck, or the experimenter's whim than they do in situations where they perceive that skill or their own characteristics determine whether or not reinforcements will occur. This idea that learning will be different under these two conditions arises naturally from the social learning theory described earlier. What is important is the *expectancy* that the behavior will lead to the reinforcement. It similarly follows in social learning theory that if one individual is subjected to a series of situations in which he has less control than another, then these expectancies for lack of control would become generalized, at least to some degree. Consequently, there may well be significant and important individual differences in the degree to which people see their own lives as determined by their own behavior and characteristics or see their lives as controlled by luck, chance, fate, or powerful others. In other words, people may differ along the dimension of a generalized expectancy (p. 105) for internal versus external control of reinforcement. If such differences do exist, identifying people and the experiences they have had which led to these differences could be of enormous practical significance in our society. It seems logical that the belief that one's own efforts can produce changes is an important ingredient in getting people to better their lives, whether in the areas of adjustment, achievement, ecology, politics, or social living.

Because of its potential applicability to so many human problems, the concept of internal versus external control of reinforcement has been investigated in literally hundreds of psychological studies. These investigations provide a dramatic example of how a theoretically based concept, originally studied under carefully controlled laboratory conditions, can lead to a variety of significant applications.

In order to study individual differences, a forced-choice scale (the I-E scale) was developed for adults by Rotter (1966) and his colleagues after refinement of a series of previous tests. Most of the research on individual differences in the control variable with adults has been based on this scale. Several other tests have since been developed for both adults and children. The four studies to be described below illustrate the range of problems which have been studied.

In an early study, Gore and Rotter (1963) set out to test the hypothesis that if people have a greater belief that their behavior determines what happens to them, then they would be more likely to take part in social action for change when they were dissatisfied with present conditions. To test this proposition, the investigators gave the I-E scale to students in a southern black college early in the semester. The subjects were students in some psychology courses during the time when there was considerable civil rights activity going on in the South. Later in the semester, just before vacation, the investigator went back to the same classes with a questionnaire about civil rights activities which the students might be willing to commit themselves to during the vacation. On this questionnaire students supplied their names and telephone numbers and signed the statements, so that there was a strong commitment being made by them to take part in the activities to which they agreed. They were given the choice of attending a rally, taking part in a march on the state capitol, joining a freedom riders group, or doing none of these. It was also possible to determine whether or not the subjects returned the questionnaire since the classes were small and it was possible to keep a record of attendance.

At this time, for a black person to take part in a march on the state capitol or a freedom ride represented not only a high degree of social action taking but a considerable risk of physical harm or imprisonment as well. The mean I-E scores for students in two groups were compared: (1) those who did not turn in their questionnaire at all, or who turned it in and had marked that they were unwilling to take part in any of the activities, or who were *only* willing to take part in a rally on campus, and, (2) those subjects who were either willing to go on a freedom ride or take part in a march on the state capitol. Students in the last two categories were significantly more internal on the I-E scale than those in the former categories. Since these were all black students who must have had high involvement in the integration issue, the results support the conclusion that people who are more internal are more likely than externals to take part in activities to change the environment when they consider it noxious.

This study was supported by Strickland (1965). In the Gore and Rotter study, while there was strong indication that the students who signed up for these activities expected to take part in them, no follow-ups were made as to whether or not they actually did. Strickland compared activists in the black civil rights movement to black people who were matched for education, socioeconomic status, and church membership, but who did not take part in civil rights activities. She again found a significant difference, with activists scoring as more internal on the I-E scale. Other studies have shown that differences in I-E scores, in comparable populations, are only minimally related or not at all related to variables such as intelligence or political preference.

It is common in our society to try to control the behavior of others by subtle or overt suggestion. Gore (1962) studied the question of how internal and external subjects reacted to these two kinds of suggestion. Gore used three groups of subjects, presenting each one with a slightly different influence situation. She had her subjects tell stories to Thematic Apperception Test pictures, telling them that she wanted to discover which pictures produced the longest stories. One group was a *control group* who presumably were not subjected to any influence. A second group was an *overt-influence group*; Gore told these subjects, as she handed them a particular picture, that she thought that this picture produced the longest and best stories. A third group was a *subtle-influence group* in which she presented the same card, smiling and saying to the subjects, "Now let's see what you do with *this* one." Her subjects had been given the I-E scale during the first day of class along with other tests, and the personality testing was not connected with the experimental situation.

Her results showed no significant differences between internals and externals—that is, between subjects divided into internal and external groups at the median of the distribution of I-E scores—in either the control condition or in the overt-suggestion condition. However, in the subtle-influence condition the internals told significantly *shorter* stories than did the externals or control subjects. In other words, under the subtle-suggestion condition, the internals were negativistic, telling stories that were even shorter than in the no-influence condition. However, in the overt-influence condition there were no traces of this negativism. Apparently, when given the conscious choice, the internal individual is not resistive; however, when he is aware that an attempt is being made to subtly manipulate him, he does become resistive.

Studies by Strickland (1970) and Getter (1966) similarly demonstrate resistiveness of internals to verbal conditioning, a subtle form of influence, when the internal subjects are aware that the experimenter is trying to manipulate them.

If internal subjects are more likely to make efforts to change the environment in a favorable direction for themselves, are they also more likely to be more effective than external subjects in such efforts? Phares (1965) attempted to answer this question by selecting a group of internal and a group of external subjects to act as experimenters in trying to change a social attitude (toward sororities and fraternities) of others. On the basis of the I-E scale, he selected a group of male internals and a group of male externals who were at the extremes of a distribution of scores. These subject-experimenters were assigned to change the opinions of a group of female students with regard to their attitudes toward fraternities and sororities. An attitude test was given before the experiment and once again afterwards. The internal and external subject-experimenters were matched for their own attitudes toward sororities and fraternities, and they were given a standard set of arguments which they were to read to subjects. Thus, the differences in their attempts to influence others were not in the content of what they said or the nature of their private opinions but in differences in voice, gestures, enthusiasm, and so on. Subjects who were assigned to the internal subject-experimenters changed their attitudes in the direction of the arguments of the subject-experimenter significantly more so than did the subjects who had external subject-experimenters and also more than did a control group, who merely took the test at the same original time and again at the same time when it was given after the experimental influence-change situation.

A somewhat different application of the concept of internal versus external control was made in a nationwide survey of the achievement of disadvantaged minority groups. This survey included thousands of children in all parts of the country.

The survey, which was conducted by a large number of social scientists, studied the relationship of school achievement to a variety of factors involving geography, school buildings, curriculum, teachers, composition of classes, and so on. Also included were "attitudinal" or personality measures of the children. A final report of this study is now known as the Coleman Report (1966).

One of the major variables investigated was the child's sense of control of the environment, which was measured by a series of questions administered to children in grades 6, 9, and 12. Among the disadvantaged children of minority groups, a strong relationship was found between the sense of control and actual school achievement. The effects were large and consistent at all three grade levels. Furthermore, the amount of variance in achievement which was accounted for by this variable was much larger than that accounted for by variations in facilities and curriculums in different schools, and, in general, more than that accounted for by any educational variable. The attitudes of internality or externality also seem to be independent of formal school characteristics and, by implication, appear to reflect home background experiences. In their summary, Coleman et al. state, "For example, a pupil attitude factor, which appears to have a stronger relationship to achievement than do all the school factors together, is the extent to which an individual feels that he has some control over his own destiny" (p. 23).

The findings of the Coleman Report are not surprising. If a minority group member feels that he cannot better himself because the world offers him no opportunity, and that powerful others are controlling what happens to him, it is not likely that he will strive very hard in school for academic achievements which he feels will not help him when he leaves school.

11

Overview

PERSONALITY AND THE SOCIAL SCIENCES

How is the study of personality related to the other social sciences? Like personality psychologists, other social scientists are also interested in predicting human behavior. The political scientist wants to know how the individual is going to vote; the sociologist is concerned with how he is affected by the norms and behavior of groups; the cultural anthropologist may focus on how he is affected by culture and changes in the culture. Within psychology, personality characteristics are important predictors of behavior for those people who are interested in education, motivation, responses to group influence, clinical problems, human engineering, and industrial psychology.

It seems clear that there is a common core to the social sciences, in that they are all concerned with the acquired or partially acquired goal-directed behavior of people. While some social sciences focus on particular kinds of problems, such as the adjustment of humans to machines, and others are interested in the behavior of groups, it seems clear that the theories and data from one social science potentially have much to offer to other social sciences. Any consistent knowledge acquired from research based on such theories would have important implications for all the social sciences. At the present time, the influence of personality characteristics tends to be ignored or minimized by those working in other areas of psychology. Experimental psychologists who are interested in human learning, perception, and problem solving must sooner or later recognize that vast individual differences exist among people and that some of these differences fall within the realm of personality psychology.

The differences among these various approaches to human behavior lie in the size and nature of the units they work with (single individuals, small face-to-face groups, large groups such as labor unions, or entire nations) and the problems they seek to solve. To the extent that they deal with different units and different problems and arise from different historical antecedents, the various social sciences tend to be organized around different constructs. That is, both in the past and in the present, social scientists have found different kinds of abstractions useful in trying to solve problems or questions that they are interested in.

In studying personality, it is often useful to borrow ideas from learning theory, perception theory, sociology, anthropology, and other areas related to the social sciences. The concept of reinforcement (borrowed from learning theory) or the concept of contrast effect (borrowed from studies of perception) are crucial in understanding how individuals acquire and change their relatively stable characteristics. If we are interested in understanding a particular individual, it is useful to know his cultural background, whether he is middle-class or lower-class, his religious background, and so on. On the other hand, social scientists working in other fields will find it valuable to use concepts which have been found useful in the study of individual differences in personality—for example, concepts dealing with defensive behavior. They may also find it necessary to describe the groups of subjects they are studying according to differences in their goals or motivations.

In other words, the social sciences do borrow from each other liberally, although each may have a unique set of abstractions or constructs developed originally to solve particular problems of interest. Interdisciplinary research approaches to solving social problems have frequently been attempted. In such approaches some combination of clinical psychologists, personality psychologists, social psychologists, sociologists, and cultural anthropologists collaborate in attacking a problem. Such approaches sometimes fail and sometimes succeed, often depending on whether they are integrating their separate approaches or merely using different words to describe the same basic variables. Richard Jessor (1968) and his co-workers have had good success in predicting particular deviant behaviors (delinquency and alcoholism) by combining constructs from personality theory, sociology, and cultural anthropology. To predict the frequency of such deviant behavior, they have used personality concepts—such as the discrepancy between an individual's goals and his expectancies of reaching them, and expectancies for internal versus external control of reinforcement—along with sociological and cultural variables which describe the opportunity structure and social acceptability of both deviant and alternative nondeviant behavior.

In addition to the commonalities in abstractions and explanations, there are methodological commonalities shared by many of the social sciences, since data are often collected from individuals in the form of verbal responses. Not only is this true of many branches of psychology but also of fields such as economics and political science, where basic data for prediction are obtained from surveys of attitudes and intentions. Perhaps more so than scientists in any other field, personality psychologists have studied in detail the problems associated with making predictions from verbal responses. Because of their extensive research into the development of predictive measures of personality, they have developed a great deal of sophistication about the motives of people responding to questionnaires, self-ratings, and so on. The many studies of the reliability and validity of measures of personality have direct application to other kinds of measures of social behavior. For example, just as one can change the percentage of people endorsing an item in a personality questionnaire by a slight change in wording, one can similarly change the percentage of people agreeing or disagreeing with a referendum question on a ballot or an opinion poll question by means of a slight change in wording. The same issue stated on a ballot will produce a different percentage of agreement if the potential voter has to vote "yes" in order to change a law or to vote "no" in order to change the same law. Similarly, the question, "Do you think the President is doing a good job?" will probably produce more agreement than the question, "Are you satisfied with the job the President is doing?" on an opinion poll.

While these important commonalities exist among the social sciences, they are often obscured by the fact that each discipline tends to develop and use its own specialized terminology, and *within* each social science competing theories use different sets of constructs or terms. The result is that it is difficult for one social scientist to learn much about other fields and their potential value to him. Eventually, it is hoped, the common core in the social sciences will be recognized and all of the fields will experience a leap forward in their understanding and prediction of human behavior.

THE PRESENT STATUS OF PERSONALITY STUDY

At this time, the greatest value of personality theories is heuristic. That is, they serve to focus interest in specific areas of research, and this leads to the systematic accumulation of new data. In themselves, however, current theories are not highly predictive. Only under carefully controlled laboratory conditions and only for particular kinds of experimental problems is it likely that consistent, highly accurate, individual predictions can be made. Even in these instances, slight variations in experimental procedures may produce unanticipated and confusing results.

This lack of validity is not surprising in that almost all theories lack one or more of the necessary components for a predictive system that can be applied to complex social behavior. These components are (1) a system of fully operationalized, carefully related constructs, (2) a sound process theory for explaining how relatively stable characteristics are acquired and changed, (3) a set of content categories for describing individual differences, and (4) a set of content categories for describing psychological situations which interact with stable personality characteristics.

The "literary" (as opposed to research-oriented) tradition in the field of personality theorizing is still strong. This tradition is exemplified in this book by several of the authors described in the early chapters. These theorists were concerned primarily with global insights into human nature. Such theories are more oriented toward generalized descriptions of broad characteristic attitudes and behaviors than toward the development of scientific terminology aimed at testing theoretical hypotheses under controlled conditions which meet stringent experimental criteria.

Nevertheless, many personality psychologists are moving away from such literary interpretations. There is growing recognition that the problem of adequately describing personality is highly complex. A few variables based on types of psychopathology are not sufficient for describing the complex nature of human beings, for predicting specific behaviors, or for understanding the many forms of maladjustment. In addition, many theorists now realize that the complex psychological situations in which people find themselves and which influence their attitudes and behaviors can no longer be ignored. Rather, the psychological situation must be treated as a major systematic variable instead of as a source of error in prediction.

Regardless of whether we are dealing with a research-oriented theory or a theory which attempts to specify the major variables determining or controlling human behavior, if there is to be any agreement among scientists and any advances in our understanding and prediction of human behavior, we need to continue to develop ways of measuring personality variables. In Chapter 9 we have described many of the methods now available. During the last twenty years, methods have become more sophisticated and potentially more useful. However, many of the tests that are now being used were developed either before the acquisition of new knowledge about test construction methodology or without regard to this new knowledge. This is not surprising—there is always a lag in science between the development of new knowledge and the application of that knowledge to specific problems.

The science of personality is still in its infancy. Psychologists who are working in this area are beginning to use a common language so that knowledge acquired in the study of such variables as aggression, anxiety, internal versus external control of reinforcement, and so on, can gradually be integrated to produce broad principles. Better ways of measuring individual differences are also developing. The future holds considerable promise for a gradual but substantial increase in our understanding of human beings.

References

Adler, A. *The practice and theory of individual psychology.* New York: Harcourt, Brace and Company, Inc., 1924.

Adler, A. *Social interest: A challenge to mankind.* New York: G. P. Putnam's Sons, 1939.

Berkowitz, L. *Aggression: A social psychological analysis.* New York: McGraw-Hill Book Company, Inc., 1962.

Boroto, D. R. The Mosher Forced Choice Inventory as a predictor of resistance to temptation. Unpublished master's thesis, University of Connecticut, 1970.

Brown, J. S., & Farber, I. E. Emotions conceptualized as intervening variables. *Psychological Bulletin,* 1951, **48,** 465–495.

Chodorkoff, B. Self-perception, perceptual defense, and adjustment. *Journal of Abnormal and Social Psychology,* 1954, **49,** 508–512.

Coleman, J. S., et al. *Equality of Educational opportunity.* Washington, D. C.: U. S. Government Printing Office, 1966.

Crandall, V. J. An investigation of the specificity of reinforcement of induced frustration. *Journal of Social Psychology,* 1955, **41,** 311–318.

Dollard, J., Doob, L. W., Miller, N. E., Mowrer, O. H., & Sears, R. R. *Frustration and aggression.* New Haven: Yale University Press, 1939.

Dollard, J., & Miller, N. W. *Personality and psychotherapy: An analysis in terms of learning, thinking, and culture.* New York: McGraw-Hill Book Company, Inc., 1950.

Epstein, S. The measurement of drive and conflict in humans. In M. R. Jones (Ed.), *Nebraska Symposium on Motivation.* Lincoln, Neb., University of Nebraska Press, 1962.

Erikson, E. H. *Childhood and society.* (2nd ed.) New York: W. W. Norton & Company, 1963.

Erikson, E. H. *Insight and responsibility.* New York: W. W. Norton & Company, 1964.

Erikson, E. H. *Identity: Youth and crisis.* New York: W. W. Norton & Company, 1968.

Freud, S. *Beyond the pleasure principle.* London, Vienna: The International Psychoanalytical Press, 1922.

Freud, S. *The basic writings of Sigmund Freud.* New York: Modern Library, 1938.

Freud, S. The psychopathology of everyday life. In J. Strachey (Ed.), *The standard edition of the complete psychological works.* Vol. 6. London: Hogarth Press, 1960.

Getter, H. A. A personality determinant of verbal conditioning. *Journal of Personality,* 1966, **34,** 397–405.

Gore, P. M. Individual differences in the prediction of subject compliance to experimenter bias. Unpublished doctoral dissertation, The Ohio State University, 1962.

Gore, P. M., & Rotter, J. B. A personality correlate of social action. *Journal of Personality,* 1963, **31,** 58–64.

Hall, C. S. *A primer of Freudian psychology.* Cleveland: World Publishing Company, 1954.

Hall, C. Strangers in dreams: An empirical confirmation of the Oedipus complex. *Journal of Personality,* 1963, **31,** 336–345.

Hamsher, J. H., Geller, J. D., & Rotter, J. B. Interpersonal trust, internal-external control and the Warren Commission Report. *Journal of Personality and Social Psychology,* 1968, **9,** 210–215.

Harlow, H. F. The formation of learning sets. *Psychological Review,* 1949, **56,** 51–65.

Henry, E., & Rotter, J. B. Situational influences on Rorschach responses. *Journal of Consulting Psychology,* 1956, **20,** 457–462.

Hochreich, D. J., & Rotter, J. B. Have college students become less trusting? *Journal of Personality and Social Psychology,* 1970, **15,** 211–214.

Jessor, R., Graves, T. D., Hanson, R. C., & Jessor, S. L. *Society, personality, and deviant behavior: A study of a tri-ethnic community.* New York: Holt, Rinehart & Winston, Inc., 1968.

Katz, H. A., & Rotter, J. B. Interpersonal trust scores of college students and their parents. *Child Development,* 1969, **40,** 657–661.

Lazarus, R. S., & Alfert, E. Short circuiting of threat by experimentally altering cognitive appraisal. *Journal of Abnormal and Social Psychology,* 1964, **69,** 195–205.

McCord, W., McCord, J., & Howard, A. Familial correlates of aggression in nondelinquent male children. *Journal of Abnormal and Social Psychology,* 1961, **62,** 79–93.

Mandler, G., & Sarason, S. B. A study of anxiety and learning. *Journal of Abnormal and Social Psychology,* 1952, **47,** 166–173.

Mandler, G., & Watson, D. L. Anxiety and the interruption of behavior. In E. D. Spielberger (Ed.), *Anxiety and behavior.* New York: Academic Press, 1966.

Maslow, A. H. *Toward a psychology of being.* Princeton, N. J.: D. Van Nostrand Company, Inc., 1962.

Maslow, A. H. *Motivation and personality.* (2nd ed.) New York: Harper & Row, 1970.

Mosher, D. L., Mortimer, R. L., & Grebel, M. Verbal aggressive behavior in delinquent boys. *Journal of Abnormal Psychology,* 1968, **73,** 454–460.

Moss, H. A. The influences of personality and situational cautiousness on conceptual behavior. *Journal of Abnormal and Social Psychology,* 1961, **63,** 629–635.

Mowrer, O. H. *Learning theory and personality dynamics.* New York: Ronald Press, 1950.

Murray, H. A. Thematic Apperception Test manual. Cambridge, Mass.: Harvard University Press, 1943.

Mussen, P. H., & Naylor, H. K. The relationship between overt and fantasy aggression. *Journal of Abnormal and Social Psychology,* 1954, **49,** 235–240.

Mussen, P. H., & Scodel, A. The effects of sexual stimulation under varying conditions on TAT sexual responsiveness. *Journal of Consulting Psychology,* 1955, **19,** 90.

Phares, E. J. Internal-external control as a determinant of amount of social influence exerted. *Journal of Personality and Social Psychology,* 1965, **2,** 642–647.

Rank, O. *Will therapy.* New York: Alfred A. Knopf, Inc., 1936.

Rapaport, D. The structure of psychoanalytic theory. In S. Koch (Ed.), *Psychology: A study of a science.* Vol. 3. New York: McGraw-Hill Book Company, Inc., 1959.

Rogers, C. R. *Client-centered therapy: Its current practice, implications, and theory.* Boston, Houghton Mifflin, 1951.

Rogers, C. R. A theory of therapy, personality, and interpersonal relationships, as developed in the client-centered framework. In S. Koch (Ed.), *Psychology: A study of a science.* Vol. 3. New York: McGraw-Hill Book Company, Inc., 1959.

Rogers, C. R. *On becoming a person.* Boston: Houghton Mifflin, 1961.

Rotter, J. B. *Social learning and clinical psychology.* Englewood Cliffs, N. J.: Prentice-Hall, Inc., 1954.

Rotter, J. B. The role of the psychological situation in determining the direction of human behavior. In M. R. Jones (Ed.), *Nebraska Symposium on Motivation.* Lincoln, Neb.: University of Nebraska Press, 1955.

Rotter, J. B. An analysis of Adlerian psychology from a research orientation. *Journal of Individual Psychology,* 1962, **18,** 3–11.

Rotter, J. B. Generalized expectancies for internal versus external control of reinforcement. *Psychological Monographs,* 1966, **80,** (1, Whole No. 609).

Rotter, J. B. A new scale for the measurement of interpersonal trust. *Journal of Personality,* 1967, **35,** 651–665. (a)

Rotter, J. B. Personality Theory. In H. Helson and W. Bevan (Eds.), *Theories and data in psychology.* New York: D. Van Nostrand Company, 1967. (b)

Rotter, J. B. Generalized expectancies for interpersonal trust. *American Psychologist,* 1971, **26,** 443–452.

Rotter, J. B., Chance, J. E., & Phares, E. J. *Applications of a social learning theory of personality.* New York: Holt, Rinehart & Winston, Inc., 1972.

Sarason, S. B., & Mandler, G. Some correlates of test anxiety. *Journal of Abnormal and Social Psychology,* 1952, **47,** 810–817.

Schachter, S. *The psychology of affiliation.* Stanford, Calif.: Stanford University Press, 1959.

Spence, K. W., & Taylor, J. A. The relation of conditioned response strength to anxiety in normal, neurotic, and psychotic subjects. *Journal of Experimental Psychology,* 1953, **45,** 265–272.

Spielberger, C. D. *Anxiety and behavior.* New York: Academic Press, 1966.

Strickland, B. R. The prediction of social action from a dimension of internal-external control. *Journal of Social Psychology,* 1965, **66,** 353–358.

Strickland, B. R. Individual differences in verbal conditioning, extinction, and awareness. *Journal of Personality,* 1970, **38,** 364–378.

Symonds, P. M. *Diagnosing personality and conduct.* New York: Appleton-Century, 1931.

Name Index

Adler, A., 21, 22, 50–66, 67, 70, 85, 91, 97, 107, 108

Berkowitz, L., 144, 157–159
Boroto, D. R., 144, 163
Brown, J. S., 144

Chance, J., 112
Chodorkoff, B., 75–77
Coleman, J. S., 168
Crandall, V. J., 110–111

Dollard, J., 94, 144
Doob, L. W., 153

Epstein, S., 147–148
Erikson, E. H., 21, 22, 42

Faber, I. E., 144
Freud, S., 11, 21, 22–41, 42, 49, 50, 60, 64, 65, 67, 73, 82, 91, 99, 145
Fromm, E., 22, 42

Geller, J. D., 161–162
Getter, H., 167–168
Gore, P. M., 165–166
Grebel, M., 156–157

Hall, C. S., 35–37
Hamsher, J. H., 161–162
Harlow, H. F., 105
Henry, E., 133–134
Hochreich, D. J., 162
Horney, K., 22, 42, 62
Howard, A., 153–155

Jessor, R., 170–171
Jung, C. G., 22

Katz, H. A., 130

Lazarus, R., 151–152

McCord, J., 153–155
McCord, W., 153–155
Mandler, G., 145–147
Maslow, A. H., 21, 80–92
Miller, N. W., 94, 144, 153
Mortimer, R. L., 156–157
Mosher, D. M., 156–157
Moss, H. A., 144, 148–151
Mowrer, O. H., 144, 153
Mussen, P. H., 134, 155–157

Naylor, H. K., 155–156

Phares, E. J., 112

Rank, O., 67–68
Rogers, C. R., 21, 67–69, 80, 85
Rotter, J. B., 21, 93–110, 149, 157, 159, 161–162, 164, 165, 166

Sarason, S. B., 145
Schachter, S., 60–62
Scodel, A., 134
Sears, R. R., 153
Spence, K. W., 144
Spielberger, C. D., 145
Strickland, B. R., 166, 167–168
Sullivan, H. S., 21, 42, 62
Symonds, P. M., 125

Taylor, J. A., 144

Watson, D. L., 145–147

179

Subject Index

2 3 4 5 6 7 8 9 10 -CP- 80 79 78 77 76 75